SHADOWS OF TIME

Jackie Meekums-Hales

Between the Lines
PUBLISHING

Willow River Press is an imprint of Between the Lines Publishing. The Willow River Press name and logo are trademarks of Between the Lines Publishing.

Between the Lines Publishing
9 North River Road, Ste 248
Auburn ME 04210
btwnthelines.com

First Published: March 2022

ISBN: (Paperback) 978-1-950502-67-7

ISBN: (Ebook) 978-1-950502-68-4

Library of Congress Control Number: 2022935794

SHADOWS OF TIME

This novel is dedicated to all those mothers and children who, in past times, have been separated by attitudes we now condemn, whether they were stolen from their rightful heritage or taken simply because their mothers were shamed into giving them up.

Einstein believed that the division of past, present, and future was an illusion.

PART ONE

"Better three hours too soon than one minute too late"
- William Shakespeare, *The Merry Wives of Windsor*

Chapter One

Scarborough seafront heaved with people enjoying the rare day of sunshine. Britain at her best, with sparkling sea, crystalized sand, and white puffs dotting the pristine blue sky. Along the harbour, fishing boats shared the dock with pleasure boats, engines at the ready, their captains plying their trade with adventurous tourists. Parents bustled towards the pirate ship, anxious to avoid cries from bored children and to give them an experience they would remember. Arcade noises sang in the background of the South Bay, as passersby ate on prawns and whelks and ice creams—determined to enjoy this day, because tomorrow could be very different.

Across the harbour, the lighthouse stood sentry, as always. Picnics dotted the colourful campsite on the beach, parents sitting as they always had on rugs, chairs, and coats—soaking up the sunshine as the sand soaked up the incoming tide. The children constructed sandcastles, paddled, and swam—searched for adventure over the rocks and in the rock pools. Safety wasn't always top priority when life had not yet shaken you. The vistas were postcards in the making—if anybody sent them anymore. Instead, social media would be full of their photos by the end of the day.

From the top of the bus, the sea looked friendly—a gentle giant sleeping, the soothing breeze a gift he blew across the land. Today the newly built, continental-coast-type apartments in the North Bay could fool you into thinking this was the Riviera of the north. Those airy balconies that beckoned you to pay for that perfect panorama screamed "newcomer misfit" at the proud old buildings along the top of the cliff. In Peasholme Park, more boats were out on the lake than had been needed for some time, and the terraces were full of those enjoying just sitting, watching, and drinking it all in. Even when the peace was shattered by the afternoon's entertainment—an organ blaring out West End music at an East End pub-like tempo—it couldn't spoil the smiles on the faces of the dads paddling away on the lake.

Everything so normal. Everyone so cheerful. Everything solid, traditional, just as it was meant to be. Except, of course, some things that weren't.

It had been a stifling few weeks—hot, sultry, storm-bidding weather, that made everyone prickly and every move a chore. There was talk of another drought as bad as 1976, but June hoped not.

At the top of the steps, near the apartments, she manoeuvred herself into a seat in the shade, content to rest here while the others ran around. The sound of her daughter's laughter forced a smile onto her molten mascara-streaked cheeks. She wiped them with a tissue as a warmth wound its way through her stomach and crept upwards to her throat.

Her son's voice, on the other hand, still took her by surprise—its depth seemingly impossible for what had been her little boy. The twins were on the brink of adulthood now, and she knew she was on borrowed time until they went their own way and left her on her own. How life had changed for all of them in the last few months! Was it better? Was it worse? She found it hard to decide.

At least they were still young enough to grab the hands of the little boy with them, running down the beach towards the water's edge. His mother watched from her towel a few yards from June's pitch.

It was a shame Libby wasn't there as well, but she'd made it clear that she did not intend to spend her summer in the UK, where it usually rained. It would be much more fun to go Interrailing with her university friends.

Was it really only a few short months since her sister had arrived at the station, eagerly scanning the crowd for the familiar face in old, familiar surroundings?

"Cathy!"

Hair sprayed into submission and make-up perfect, Cathy turned her head towards the kiosk to find her sister, bustling as ever, looking

"I can't imagine it for you, Libs. That's for sure. You need to be somewhere that suits your free spirit, not shackled to some old house and smothered in responsibility." Belle shook her head in sympathy.

"I need an escape plan as soon as I've finished uni. I didn't get a gap year like a lot of others, because we've never had any money, but once I can earn my way round the world, I'm off. Freedom, here I come!" Libby raised an arm dramatically in the air, and Belle gave her a high five as they chuckled.

"What about your brother and sister?" asked Belle, with a concerned frown.

"What about them? They seem quite content with village life, with wellie boots and dogs and horses. To use one of Grandma's expressions: they'll be as happy as pigs in muck. They're welcome to it. They can run the ancestral pile of crap that is our house, and I'll tell them how good they are at it. I'm not going to be working in the union bar forever, and I'm not going to be spending my time trying to pay off my student loan before I'm a pensioner. If my Auntie Cathy could take off for Australia and make a pile of money, why shouldn't I? Maybe she could put me up when I'm on my travels, if I can cope with her obsession with tidiness. God, she's awful! She always has to look as if she just stepped out of a magazine!"

Belle laughed with her, not daring to say that she didn't believe a word of what Libby said she was going to do. She was sure they would both finish uni and get good jobs, and life would start to weave itself into some kind of normal future. Libby was such a drama queen, though she loved her dearly.

As they tossed the pile of rejected clothes into the bottom of the wardrobe, Libby ventured in a calmer tone, "I wonder what Cathy's like now, to be honest. I hope she and Mum are getting on. They're so different! Last time I saw her for any length of time, I was fourteen, and she was a nuisance."

"Did she come for a holiday, then?"

"No. That's just it. It was when my granddad died. There was crying all over the house, what with Gran and Mum, and then Cathy joined in as well. I felt I had to be there for the twins, who'd been unusually quiet for a change, but the whole atmosphere was as if someone had thrown a dark net over the house, trapping it in a veil of grief. I missed my granddad, but I felt like I do now. I just wanted to get away from them all. No one wanted to talk about my feelings, least of all me." Libby's head dropped as she stared down at the ticket in her hand.

Belle wasn't sure how to respond as Libby slipped into silence, remembering how she didn't want to face the reality of death or to have to deal with all these grown-ups who should have been there for her but were too engrossed in their own sadness and comforting each other. Even the dogs seemed to know all was not right, as Bonzo lay down on the kitchen tiles, head on paws and eyes looking miserably upwards as though he were being soaked in a rain shower. Jupiter paced up and down, back and forth until Mum had shouted at him to "stop it, for goodness' sake!" He'd been banished to the conservatory, where he gave the occasional whine.

"What's your problem with this Cathy?" Belle dared to whisper. She sensed Libby's withdrawal.

"Oh, the perfect, preened Cathy was the outsider, yet somehow she'd made it inside, and it was me who felt as if I were looking in." Libby lifted her head, looking straight into Belle's eyes with an honesty that stripped away the drama of her declaration. "I didn't dare say it, but I was glad when she went back to Australia! I'm glad I'll be able to come straight back to my room in halls after the funeral this time, so that I don't have to deal with the rest of them and I can get on with my own life."

Libby resented the fact that Cathy had no idea what they'd dealt with since she went back to her perfect life. They were the ones who'd seen Maggie struggle to cope with losing the man she'd shared her life with. They were the ones who heard her crying when she thought they couldn't hear, the ones who sorted the paperwork, the bills, the things that went wrong, the gradual memory loss that began to rob Maggie of her lifestyle. What did Cathy know, when all she'd done was phone every few weeks to be told everything was fine? Occasionally she'd manage to get Maggie onto Skype, where the older woman would put on a brave face and smile and chatter as if nothing were wrong. It was so easy to pretend when someone wasn't there all the time. Libby knew it was June who had shouldered the worry and care, who watched the slow decline of the mother she loved so much.

Maggie had been such a vital person—always going somewhere, doing something, or helping someone else—but she'd slowly become a prisoner in her own home, afraid of a world advancing without her, mystified by technology she could no longer keep up with and baffled by the memory loss that dogged her last year. If that was what getting old meant, Libby didn't want it. She was reminded of a poem she'd studied in school, saying: "Let me die a young man's death". Being mown down by a car at the age of seventy-three, shot by gangsters at the age of ninety-one, or murdered at the age of one hundred and four may have been funny at the time, but now, oh now, she knew what McGough meant—anything but that slow descent in nothingness.

Libby glanced around her room to make sure she had everything she needed to take home, turning her back on the pile of clutter on her desk, and set off for the station. In her rucksack was her iPad, on which she'd stored the results of the DNA test she sent off for analysis online.

It had started as a kind of joke between her and her friends, one of whom also had ginger hair. After an evening of a few too many shots, they thought it would be fun to see whether the theory was true: Are we never that far away from someone we're distantly related to, and are we really connected to everyone through just a few people? Maybe they were both descended from Vikings. Maybe they were related to each other. The test was on special offer, so what harm could it do? It was just a bit of fun. She doubted that it would ever come to anything. Results might even suggest she had some distant relatives out there, but she certainly didn't intend to contact all the people who'd been identified as things like fourth cousins. It might amuse the family on a different occasion, but now was not that time.

Libby's arrival was, as usual, a whirlwind affair—doors flinging open and overjoyed dogs trying to wake up the whole village. The furry beasts would rush at her, knowing she would drop to her knees to make a fuss of them before she did anything else. A rucksack was pushed into the kitchen ahead of her, like an uninvited guest. She was only staying for two nights, even though she dumped a huge holdall full of what her mother knew was probably mostly dirty washing on the kitchen floor.

June called from the stairs, the grin on her face audible in her voice, "Welcome home, number one! Put the washing in the utility room."

"Hi, Mum! What have we got for lunch?" came the usual reply.

Each time she returned, they played out the same scene, greeting each other with practicalities that belied the joy they had in being in the same house again. June could never tell Libby how she cried all the way home when she left her oldest daughter on the steps of the halls of residence. Libby would never admit to June that she had been so scared of her new-found independence, finding new friends, managing to live on what she had. The big, wide world was full of surprises, not all of them good. For each of them, there'd been a time of adjusting to the other's absence, but Libby had soon found herself one of a group of girls on the same floor, sharing a kitchen and learning to leave their washing-up at their peril because here there was no one to do it for you. June wondered if it was the same for all mothers, that gut-wrenching loss of closeness that she once had with her oldest child.

Libby knew she'd been more than a daughter. When there were just the three of them years ago—Libby, Mark, and June—Mark had doted on his firstborn in a way he would never dote on the twins, whose sleepless nights were often avoided when he flew across the world to the next conference or contract work. Libby had been June's companion on those lonely nights when Mark came home late or not at all. She'd been her pal when they jumped in puddles or danced to the latest hit. She'd been her sidekick when the twins had arrived, and two hands were just never enough. She filled June with pride time and time again, with work displayed on the classroom wall or being an angel in the nativity play, to growing into someone full of compassion for animals and humans. Her strong sense of right and wrong impelled her towards causes to be fought, and June had often suggested she might go into politics.

Instead, Libby had chosen medicine, though no one in the family had ever been a medic. The closest was her grandfather, who'd been a vet. Her mother had often told them tales of how he would be called out to deal with some lamb in the freezing February snow or some poor horse, injured at the racecourse or in the hunt. They'd been assured that being a vet was not about fluffy cats and docile dogs, and Libby's love of animals didn't extend to wanting to have to learn how to fix them all. She was, at least, only dealing with one species, and that had been more than enough.

In her first year, Libby felt like giving up altogether. There was so much to learn, and there were so many students from private schools—where they had achieved more A's than she had at A level—that she felt she couldn't compete. She'd stuck her colour-coded notes all round her room, drumming into her head a whole new vocabulary, more like learning a foreign language than learning scientific fact.

This year had got off to a better start, as she'd matched and outshone most of them. By the end of last year, she'd begun to love what she was doing. She'd mastered the decoding of the textbooks. Now, she was focused and determined, and she would succeed, however much hard work it took. She couldn't wait to be let loose on a hospital, dealing with real people all the time, instead of theory.

As Libby put the kettle on and moved quietly around the kitchen, hunting out biscuits and buns, the twins arrived home from school.

"Libby!" exclaimed Millie, throwing herself into her sister's open arms.

Alex followed, a little more sedately, as befitted his burgeoning manhood. He gave her a hug and a peck on the cheek before stepping back to flick his hair and ask her how she was doing. His voice sounded deep and seemed unreal—so weirdly like her dad's.

"I'm fine, little brother, thanks. What about you? Got a girlfriend yet?"

Alex winced, as if he had been stung by a bee. "Too many women in my life already," he quipped, turning quickly so she couldn't see the blush that crept to his face from his neck.

Chapter Four

Cathy managed not to say how much Libby had grown, but she couldn't help noticing that the girl she'd seen on her last visit was now very much a young woman with a style all her own. There was definitely something of her mother's organised chaos about her, though with her generous mouth and Roman nose, she looked more like her father in some ways. She spent her time catching up with her siblings, teasing Alex about girls, and sharing wardrobe disasters with Millie. She was polite when Cathy asked her how she was, but there was no warmth. It was almost as though she resented Cathy's presence and her importance to June, as though she was the one who made June cry when Libby needed her mother to stay the strong, independent woman she could rely on. It was obvious, in her body language, that the multiplied grief generated when the two sisters were together was more than Libby wanted to deal with.

The church was full on the day of the funeral. Maggie had been a regular at Sunday services and had kept the altar supplied with greenery and flowers from the smallholding. She'd belonged to the local Women's Institute. She'd helped at the village hall events and rallied troops for manning stalls for the annual fete. Some cursed her as she approached and tried to persuade them to do something or buy something, but most knew her, and many had her to thank for knowing each other.

The vicar gave a heartfelt eulogy, including in it the tributes June and Cathy made to their mother. With her gentle encouragement and unselfish, unstinting support, the sisters realised, as adults, that their mother had been their biggest inspiration.

Some contributions to the eulogy by others were hardly recognisable to June and Cathy—a saintly personification of the person they had just known as a mother. Neither of them had felt able to read anything aloud themselves, and they reached for each other's hands, as the vicar began:

"Maggie Mitchell was someone we all knew as a pillar of village life in this place that she loved and where she had lived all her youth and adulthood. She will be sadly missed by so many people, in so many different ways, and today we gather together to celebrate a life that has touched ours and others.

"Maggie was born in 1926, in the middle of the General Strike. She grew up a much-loved daughter of the local vet, and she was very close to her late brother. Like others of her age, her teenage years were blighted by the onset of war, and many of you will know that the trading estate was then an airfield, so planes would have been flying overhead throughout the years of conflict. Her old school friend, Eileen, has written her own tribute, which I will read to you:

I knew Maggie from the day we started at the village school—when we still had one. We walked together every day, until bright girl that she was, she gained a well-deserved place at the local grammar school and my parents sent me away to board, but that could not break a friendship that survived everything life threw at us, despite losing touch for a while at the end of the war.

She loved to dance, and she had a quick sense of humour. She was a beautiful child, admired by everyone, and she was always a good person. I don't remember her ever being in trouble, and she was kind, even when very young.

She cried with me when my daughter was in hospital. She worked tirelessly for charity, especially charities to help children, and she was always there if someone was going through a hard time or needed a friendly face. She gathered up new people in the village, introducing them to others and helping them to settle in.

She didn't make a fuss about what she did, as she was one of those people who beaver away in the background, never seeking thanks. She loved her husband and children, who were the centre of her world, and she was happiest when she could get them all together. Sam idolised her, and their marriage lasted over 50 years, leaving her desolate when he died. Inside the Maggie of recent years was the girl I remember, and the world has lost a very special person.'"

The vicar then read a few short tributes, passed on by neighbours and other members of the community, but by then June and Cathy were hardly able to hear them. It was as if they were listening to a tribute to someone they had never known, someone with a life that reached out beyond them and that stretched back to a time before they even existed.

Cathy felt a sob begin to climb up to her throat, and it took all the will she could muster to force it back down. June was quietly crying into her crumpled tissue as Libby's arm crept round her shoulders. The twins, she noticed, were looking at the floor, avoiding the coffin in front of them. Cathy found herself envying June her daughter's comfort.

To the sisters, Maggie had just been their mother, but they heard about what she had been to so many other people, how she'd laughed with them, cried with them, helped them, and once upon a time been young and had fun with them. None of these people seemed to know the depression her daughters sometimes sensed in her, the way she could be stubborn and awkward, how angry she got about some things, or how she had struggled after their father died. Only now would missing her make them truly appreciate all she had been to them and all she had done for them.

June looked at all the flowers spread out for the family to see and wondered about how many people her mother had been. She would have said they should have a charity collection instead, but they'd been too preoccupied to think about it. There were kind exchanges at the wake, and several of June's friends had made the effort to come support her. Cathy had met them before, so she put on her polite face to welcome Julia and Steven, both June's teaching colleagues.

"We're so sorry to hear about the sudden departure," offered Julia, Steven echoing her in the background. "I lost my own mother last year, so I know just how you must be feeling." She put a sympathetic hand on Cathy's arm.

What were you supposed to say on these occasions? Part of Cathy wanted to scream at them all, "Why are you here? Why don't you just all leave us to grieve, instead of making us socialise when we want to curl up and cry?" She managed a weak smile of appreciation and excused herself on the pretence of needing to find June.

June was standing by the kitchen door, trapped by another couple wanting to talk about what had happened. She recognised these two as Felicity and Jeremy, whom June had met at the twins club when Alex and Millie were babies. From what she remembered from her last visit, their boys were keen on rugby and destined to row for Oxford, if their father's aspirations were realised.

Cathy gave them a small wave as she veered towards the dining room where she could escape through the French doors and head for the summer house to take herself in hand. She desperately wished Karen or Sally were here, so she had someone to share her thoughts with. If only she weren't single again... Loneliness circled her like a predator sizing up its prey, waiting to pounce whenever her guard was down.

After several minutes and a fleeting wish that she still smoked— her teenage experiment having left her with nothing but distaste—she walked round to the kitchen door and let herself in. She lifted a plate of sandwiches from the worktop and into the air, ensuring that she could not be expected to stand still and engage in conversation with people that were now only seen at family funerals.

One of them was their cousin Ed Harrison. Ed was a strange man. He and his wife usually stayed for no longer than was necessary to have met their obligations and took their leave, but today they lingered until they could catch June on her own, on her way out to the kitchen with some empty plates.

"June," said a familiar voice from her right elbow, surprising her with its voluntary approach. As she turned to look at him, June noticed that even with age, his beautiful eyelashes, soft mouth, and delicate hands seemed more appropriate for a model than an accountant, though time had increased his waistline and furrowed his brow.

"Ed, thank you so much for coming. I hope you're well."

"I'm fine, thanks. I just wanted to say how bad my father felt about the house being left only to him." June knew Ed was referring to the house that Maggie grew up in. It, along with the neighbouring veterinary practice, had been purposely kept out of Maggie's inheritance, and Ed had chosen to abandon his father's profession. "He always felt their father never quite forgave your mother," Ed went on, "you know, for the transgressions of her youth. Such a shame." Although his accent reflected his Cambridge education, his gruff tone, so unlike his father's, was that of a man with few social graces.

Suddenly, June was really listening. Almost laughing at the thought that her mother could have done anything drastically wrong, she asked, "Really, Ed? What did she do that was so awful?"

"You don't know?" His unkempt curls fell across his eyes, allowing him to avoid meeting hers.

"Know what?"

"Oh, sorry. I shouldn't have said anything. Forget it. We must be going."

"No, wait a minute, Ed. You can't leave me wondering like that. What happened? What is it I don't know?"

Ed, embarrassed and flustered, gathered up his coat and made towards the door, but June grabbed his arm while others innocently blocked his escape.

"What? Tell me!"

Ed's shoulder's slumped in defeat as he gave in. "Well, the time she spent in Wales with her aunt...A few months… Nobody was told why, but everyone knew. The shame in those days. She was lucky your father fell in love with her."

He wrenched away from June's grasp, making for a sudden gap. As people moved away from the door, Ed reached his wife and turned her on her heels, guiding her by the elbow out into the garden and round to the street. Unable to go after him without barging through guests trying to take their sympathetic leave, June was left puzzled by his insinuations. She put on a fake smile to shake the hands offered to her as she pondered his words.

Cathy had been watching from the doorway, not wanting to be drawn into a conversation with their cousin whom she remembered as someone she hadn't much liked. She raised her eyebrows as her silent question met June's puzzled face. *What just happened?* Part of her longed to mingle with these people who knew who she was, but the other part felt the estrangement of years of separation. She saw two elderly women looking sideways at her as they obviously discussed her. She could imagine the sympathetic comments, embroidered with observations on her appearance and character, compared with their memories of a Cathy she no longer knew herself. She knew there would have been whispers about why she had gone. It just wasn't what you did—leave your parents and your village and move to the other side of the world—unless something propelled you. She'd never given them the satisfaction of a reason beyond wanting an adventure. She'd kept contact with no one other than her parents, and through them, her sister. She wondered what they thought and what they were saying, but only out of curiosity. She would not engage in conversations that allowed them to ask the questions burning their tongues. Some things had not changed, and she knew they would lay claim to her as one of theirs, entitling them to show an interest in her life. She suddenly felt just as she had all those years ago, retreating inside herself and shutting the door in the face of any attempt to reach her.

Chapter Five

All around the room were sympathy cards—flowers sitting on every window ledge, on the coffee table, and even on the floor. June's eyes swept from left to right, trying to accept the finality of the funeral. The event seemed to have passed in a blur, a montage of going through the motions and doing what was expected. Her sense of unreality was all that stopped the tears from falling. With determination to reinstate some kind of stability for the children, she began to gather up the cards. June was making a stack of the melancholy floral-and-scripture-themed notes when Cathy came into the room.

"We need to clear this lot away," June said in a matter-of-fact tone, assuming the role of big sister, as she had always done. At a young age, she'd learnt to protect Cathy by hiding her own turbulent emotions. She had to be the one to turn to practicalities. Even when they were children, she was always the one who played Lady of the Manor while her sister went off on adventures. They coped with life in their different ways. "It looks like a funeral parlour with all these flowers in one room."

They bring back too many memories with you here, June thought, *like finding Mum in tears on her first Mother's Day after you left, clutching the flowers you sent. She knew you wouldn't come back. I saw the pain behind the smile and bustle, but I could never be enough to take away the sadness of you deciding to stay across the other side of the world. One piece of our family jigsaw was always missing. Now it's another piece. Why are you here now when you weren't here then?*

As June began to pile the cards on the old coffee table, she asked Cathy, "Well, what did you make of that?" her smile giving away nothing of the consternation she felt.

"Make of what?" Cathy replied, moving a vase from one ledge to another, automatically tidying.

"Our cousin turning up," June ventured, wondering how much Cathy had absorbed.

"He's a strange one, isn't he?" pondered Cathy, picking up another vase. "I could never understand why Mum always made excuses for him, could you?"

"She said he had a difficult childhood because his mother died in childbirth, leaving him to the mercies of nannies until he could be sent away to school. Apparently, he was bullied, but the reason seems to have been some kind of secret we were not to be told."

"Such a long-kept secret at that. We'll never know, I suppose, but he was never good at making friends."

I know a lot more than you do, June thought. "I guess you were too young to remember the birthday party when he was deliberately the first one out in musical chairs and pass the parcel, and then he found an excuse to leave the room when it came to apple bobbing." She forced a laugh. "He always seemed to be angry about something when he had to play with others. He still hides himself away, and I'm not convinced he ever smiles. His wife, Claire, seems pleasant enough, though; he was lucky to find her. I think they met at some society when he was a student. Shame they never had any children." She was aware that her stress was making her gabble about him, to distract her from asking what she really wanted to ask.

What did Cousin Ed mean about their mother never being forgiven by her father? June was thinking. *What had gone on between her and her brother, Matthew? They were both popular in the village, and she was devastated when he died so suddenly on his skiing trip. I know they cared about each other, but they lived different lives, and they were never very close. He was always the one with money. Mum wouldn't talk about it, but I found out through the grapevine that he got everything when Granddad died. Why? Too many unanswered questions!*

June stared at the pile of cards knowing she would have to face reading them. Cathy seemed to be hovering in a familiar way that made June wonder what she was thinking. When they were young, June had grown used to Cathy's body language, always knowing when there was something under the surface, but Cathy would need time and space to decide what and when to tell those close to her. Sometimes, it would come in an outburst—something minor pulling the trigger of the tension gun. Other times, she would be found in floods of angry tears, blurting out what had gone wrong only when she was discovered. Sometimes, June knew, she told no one anything, and the secret side of her was like their mother had been—locking things away behind an impenetrable wall of pretence that she was all right. Silence locked them in their separation.

Even if June wanted to ask Cathy about the inner workings of her mind, as the door flew open, and in bounded the dogs followed by the twins, their noise and cheerful chatter filled the room.

There was an explosion of glass crashing into stone as the dogs' irreverent pleasure at reaching June resulted in a vase of flowers and water being knocked into the hearth and Bonzo's wagging tail consigned the cards to the floor. Amid the chaos, June saw Cathy slip out of the room, one unscathed vase of flowers clutched tightly in both hands.

"What's for lunch, Mum?" Alex brought normality to June. She smiled at him and Millie and decided the mess could wait. This was home, where she grew up with the freedom of the fields and orchards. She belonged, and the children needed her to carry on, just as she had when her marriage had fallen apart. This rambling old house was her sanctuary, and it seemed the most natural thing in the world to take over running it as her mother aged. For June, living in the same place among those whose forebears had known each other and where everyone knew to which family you belonged, felt safe and comforting. Until the recent influx of new people filling the new houses, a marriage between two people still seemed to be a marriage of two families, and the traits of the young were firmly anchored in the traits of their ancestors, for good or ill. That was what she wanted for her children. Safety. Security.

Children first, June thought. *I need to keep them happy. They've had enough loss already. I worry about Libby. I know how she cried in the night when her dad went, and it's been a long road to happiness for her, especially since he remarried, but she's too much like Cathy to tell me how she's feeling now. I can't let them see me upset.* There were times when she envied her sister her freedom, but sun, sea, and money would not be enough to take her away from her family.

"As long as it's eggs, you can have what you like!" June answered, ushering them into the kitchen ahead of her. "And get those dogs into the conservatory before I fall over them!"

As she juggled scrambling and frying eggs, June realised that Cathy had not reappeared.

PART TWO

"What's in a name? That which we call a rose by any other name would smell as sweet"

- William Shakespeare, ***Romeo and Juliet***

Chapter Six

"Have you got a photo of Great-grandma?" Georgie asked innocently. "We're doing family trees at school. I need to make a list of all the surnames and all the places my ancestors came from."

Bob tried to hide the feeling that the blood was draining from his face. His heart sped up as he just managed enough control to answer. "Well, I'll have to have a think about that, young man."

He knew that fobbing off a bright seven-year-old probably wasn't going to work, but right now he didn't feel up to a full explanation.

Luckily, at that very moment, his daughter called to her son, "Georgie. You haven't cleaned your teeth yet. Hurry up! Bedtime, NOW!" When Vicky had that teacher's tone in her voice, you did as you were told, even if you were her father, so, unsurprisingly, Georgie pecked his granddad on the cheek and, with a brief "Night," disappeared from the room.

Left alone with his thoughts, Bob tried to work out what his emotions actually were. He'd never questioned his upbringing, never felt the slightest flicker of that burning desire others felt. His mother had just been his mother, the only one he ever needed. They'd been remarkably close, mother and son, with his father often away working and no sibling rivals to compete for attention. He would never have done anything to upset her, and when she'd gently told him he was adopted, it was with tears tumbling down her usually-so-brave face, assuring him what a longed-for, precious child he was, and how much she would always love him. From that day, he'd known that his real parents must have had no choice. His father had been a pilot, shot down in the last days of the war. His broken-hearted "birth mother," as they now called it, died giving birth to him a few months later, and he was left with a sad tale about strangers he had never known. So, he'd pushed it to the back of his mind, and shut it out of the reality of his life.

Bob's childhood memories were good ones that made him feel a warmth from the happiness and security he'd known. It was only last year, when his adoptive mother Peggy died, that he began to wonder about who he really was. Sorting through her bureau, feeling as if he were invading her privacy, he'd come across his adoption papers folded into a faded, yellowed envelope inside a leather pouch. What he saw bundled in a blue ribbon hit him like a cricket ball fast bowled into his chest. As he slowly pulled the ends of the baby-blue bow, the bundle tumbled out onto the bed and an envelope landed on his thigh. Beautiful italic handwriting contained just three words: *My Darling Boy*.

He trembled as he carefully lifted the flap that had been tucked into the envelope. Tentatively, he pulled out the pristine paper into daylight it hadn't seen for a very long time—sixty-four years. He knew what it was before those slow-motion seconds passed and he could read:

> *To my son, my darling boy, on this, the last day I shall hold you in my arms.*
>
> *Know that I loved you beyond measure, will always, always love and miss you for the rest of my life. If I had any way to keep you, I would, but your dear father has gone to heaven, and I must put your happiness and your future before my own. Have a wonderful life, my precious one. Maybe one day we shall see each other again.*
>
> *All my love*
>
> *Mummy xxxx*

His brain was spinning so fast he thought he would pass out. He took a deep breath. Maybe it was nothing to do with him. He looked again, but he had to acknowledge that there it was, tied with a bow to his papers. His name, as he knew it, was Robert George. Not a huge leap from that to Richard. R.G.—Peggy kept the initials.

Bob read the letter again, and again, desperately trying to make sense of what his eyes were telling him. Could his loving, caring, wonderful mother have lied to him? Could his birth mother have been out there, all this time? He didn't want to believe the gnawing sense of betrayal by the one person he had always felt he could trust. She loved him. How could she have kept this from him? Why? Was she selfish, after all, wanting him just for herself, or was she afraid? He wanted to ask her, wanted to get hold of her bony old shoulders and make her look him in the eye. But it was too late. He would never know.

Stunned, he meticulously inspected every piece of the bundle as if it were part of a crime scene. So...there it was, his real name, his real history. She hadn't died, this woman who had given him life.

He never found it necessary to complicate the lives of his own children with the details of his adoption, and they'd loved Peggy, who had been a doting grandmother. Robert senior had been a proud grandfather, who worked his magic in his old shed at the bottom of the garden, producing wooden toys that delighted the children with their novelty—little horses carved from scraps, miniature dolls that Peggy had dressed, trains and boats and planes that they could paint and zoom.

The garden had irritated Bob with its insistence on controlling nature. His dad, Robert, hadn't shared Bob's love of the great outdoors, his exhilaration at the top of rolling moors and dales. Robert thought reading Wordsworth was for sissies. Bob should want to take out a garden fork and dig. They'd laughed about it, but they both knew that somehow the absence of a genetic link blocked that empathy that comes from following in your father's footsteps—something they could never truly have, despite their acceptance of their differences and the deep bond of love between them.

And now, Georgie wanted names and places. Well, Bob couldn't give him more than one name and one place. There was no mention of the romantic pilot shot down at the end of the war. Did he exist, or was this another fabrication? These days, he knew some people were able to find their missing parentage, but when he was growing up, this had not been an option, and his birth mother could never have found him, even if she'd wanted to. As his stomach stopped churning and he was able to gather his thoughts, he realised that maybe he'd been protected from a yearning that could never be satisfied. At least thinking both his parents dead meant that Peggy had ensured he wouldn't be hurt by an impossible longing. Yet she had kept the truth hidden in the bundle she'd obviously felt unable to destroy. Maybe the next generation had a right to that truth. Maybe he did.

Back in the secret protection of his own study, he tentatively googled "family history" and began his search. He'd watched a BBC series in which famous people had traced their families back and back. He knew it sometimes gave them unpleasant surprises, but for the first time in his life he felt driven to find out something—anything—that might anchor him in a past that had so far eluded him. A visit to his local library provided him with a copy of the book based on the series, and armed with the links he needed, he shut himself away.

Several days later, and several pounds poorer, he arranged his scribbles into some kind of order. He'd found a database on one of the genealogy sites called "living relatives," hoping and dreading that her name would just pop up.

Nothing.

Of course, she might have married...but there were pages and pages of possible marriages. He tried to imagine how old she would have been. He guessed she would have been incredibly young when he was born, so maybe she was born in the 1920s. He'd heard about what happened to girls of her generation and before—ones who "got themselves into trouble". Locked away, some of them, in institutions for the insane. Others sent to have their babies away from shaming eyes, forced to submit to society's hypocrisy by giving up their child or living an outcast from "decent" people. Some, old enough to marry, would have paid a different price in a "shotgun marriage" to satisfy the demands of society, rather than marrying for love. There hadn't even been the option of divorce in an age when the woman couldn't support herself and her child. He'd been told about one of Peggy's relatives, who hit the headlines in the local newspaper for daring to be divorced in the 1940s.

Bob tried another website, this one miraculously free. He typed in her name and chose the whole decade of the twenties. *If only I knew where she came from, I could narrow it down.* He looked again at his papers. Perhaps she hadn't gone that far from home to have her baby, but she would have gone far enough to make sure no one who knew her would set eyes on her expanding shape. The letter had no address or postmark at the top, but one of the other documents was headed. That meant she had probably been somewhere in the north, and now he had an initial for her middle name. At least that narrowed down the search. He was left with two girls with the same name, born five years apart in the same area. So maybe one of these was his "mother." Nervously, he thought, *Could I really have found her?* His hands hovered over the keyboard, the merging excitement and fear like waiting for a terrifying fairground ride he couldn't resist taking.

She wouldn't have been married before he was born, so at least he had that clue when sifting through the girls' marriage records. He should be going to bed, but now this mystery had wrapped itself around his mind like a tightening python, and he couldn't stop.

One was born in 1926, the other in 1929. One was married in 1950, the other in 1946. It seemed unlikely that his mother would have married as soon as he had been despatched, so his money was on the 1950 one.

"Got it!" He jotted down the reference number. "Now I can order a copy of the certificate." That done, he finally went to bed exhausted, to dream about someone trying to snatch his grandchildren while they played because he didn't deserve them.

Chapter Seven

A few days later, the certificate dropped through the letter box. Bob hesitantly and carefully slid the letter opener under the top of the envelope. Then, there it was, in his hand.

Name of bride—Margaret Catherine Harrison, spinster.

Name of groom—Samuel Alexander Mitchell, bachelor.

Suddenly, a light shone on who they were and where they came from, as if some genie had rubbed a lamp and given him a glimpse of the past. It seemed they'd lived in the same parish before they married, and he pictured this 1950s scene: a young couple coming out of the local church smiling and happy, people throwing confetti, the bride tossing her modest bouquet, a couple of bridesmaids shivering in their pink finery on a cold January day. He imagined the groom's 1940s de-mob suit and her 50s hairstyle with a dress economic on material, but maybe still modestly long.

Did Samuel know about him? he wondered. *Had she confessed all, or was he just a secret she had kept to herself?*

Bob's eye ran along the document he held in his shaking hands, landing on the details of "father's occupation". He realised that one of these was his grandfather who had passed on genes he might have inherited. Did this man enjoy what he enjoyed? Was he good at what Bob was good at? Did he like the same things, hate the same things? Her father's name was Henry, a vet, the groom's father a farmer. Easy to see how they might have met, then. He imagined the vet's daughter brought up in a gentile household among middle-class friends. *Maybe she was swept off her feet by the dashing young pilot from the local air base, but eventually settled for the life of a farmer's wife. Maybe she met her pilot at a dance in the village hall. Maybe she had her first kiss under the moonlight just before her father came to walk her home. And she'd fallen in love in a time when no one knew how long they would live, or how many would die as sacrifices for peace. Love and war must have made young people want to live for today, while they could,* he mused.

The light was fading in the room, and he realised how long he'd sat there clutching the certificate like an Olympic medal, dreaming life into names on paper. He placed the document on the centre of the table, as if afraid that a puff of wind would steal from him this embryonic insight into the life of these people he could call family.

Suddenly, his birth mother was a real person. She never mattered before because she didn't exist, but now he would never be able to return to that comfortable space. Now, his head was filling up with a kaleidoscope of questions. *What did she look like? What kind of world did she live in where she had no choice but to give up her son and no right to find him again?* Had she just got on with her life, or had she struggled with that loss, like people he'd seen on his television screen? These days, it was clear that many young mothers gave up their babies because they had no choice in a time of dependence on parents and husbands. *And this marriage—was it love or something she settled for to give her respectability and a home?*

He was consumed by a need to know more, but where was he to start? The past as he knew it was changing and knocking on the door of the present, like an insistent visitor.

Chapter Eight

Armed with the addresses on the marriage certificate, a smartly dressed man could be seen driving at a snail's pace up and down a sodden Main Street, peering through the autumn rain at the different house numbers. The new houses fronting the road hadn't been there sixty years ago when fields and barns had stretched along the perimeter of the farm, and the old orchard had been where the new-born lambs had been fed by the children. Only the occasional apple tree gave away any clue to its existence now.

Bob had almost given up hope when he pulled up outside the post office. It was only as he clambered out of the car that he realised he was, in fact, staring at a building that had been there since the nineteenth century. The modern façade had been added some time ago, but above it were the signs of age—a slightly wonky roof line, some old gutters, and ornate chimney pots that no one would bother with now, unless it were to plant things in them. The pebble-dashed, white walls belied the old brick and cobble of the original building, and Bob decided to take a closer look. He tried to seem as if he were nonchalantly peering at the contents of the window display, fascinated by the biscuits and tins on offer, despite the rain dripping off the awning above his head. But, like an alien spy, he was taking in far more than it seemed. He scanned to the left of the shop front, where a door appeared to lead to the living accommodation. Above the door, set in a rectangle of concrete within the wall, was "Hawthorn Row".

Eureka! Bob thought triumphantly. He hadn't found Hawthorn House, but it was a pretty sure bet that it couldn't have been far away.

A few yards along the road was what looked like the access to someone's drive leading between two of the "executive homes" along the grass verge. He tried to look inconspicuous by appearing to stride confidently and purposefully into the gap, avoiding looking round to see if he was being followed, using his umbrella as a shield. A dog barked, momentarily halting him as he was approaching a huge oak tree, its rust and gold canopy dipping over the track and hiding whatever might be ahead. He took cover under its leaves and stood still, staring at the large stone-built house at the top of the drive, which opened out into a secluded, immaculately manicured front garden.

Bob was just about to give in to the rain, smother his longing to ask about the family that had lived there, when the huge front door was wrenched open, and he found himself being rounded up by a Border Collie. Its black and white head was low, and its bark threatened to drive the trespasser up the tree.

Puffing and panting came a red-faced, portly man in a checked jacket, flat cap, and green wellington boots. "Blasted Nell," he said to himself as he turned to heave closed the reluctant door as quickly as he could. It was only as he turned back and hurried down the drive, leaning on his walking stick for support, that his eyes landed first on the umbrella, then on the man frozen to the spot, with the dog pinning him to the tree trunk as surely as if he were lassoed.

"Who the hell are you?" Ed threw at Bob. "And what the hell are you doing on my drive? *Shut up, Nell.* SIT!"

Bob felt as if he should sit himself, but he took a deep breath of relief when the dog called Nell finally did as she was told, after letting out a low growl of disapproval.

"I'm so sorry," Bob began. *What could he say*, he wondered, *that wouldn't make him sound like some creepy intruder with malicious intent?* "I once knew of someone who supposedly lived here, but it was a long time ago, and I guess you wouldn't have known her. I was in the area, so I just thought I'd see where the house was..."

"I've lived here all my life, and I'd thank you to get out of my garden now that you've seen what you came to see," was the gruff rejoinder.

"Right yes, of course. Only—if you've lived here all your life, could you tell me where I might find any of the Harrison family?"

Ed spun on his heel, turning to look this stranger in the eye. "My name is Harrison. Who's asking?"

"I'm Bob Thompson." Bob reached out his hand, dropping it gently to his side as Ed ignored it. "My mother knew someone called Maggie Harrison many years ago, and she asked me if I could find out what happened to her while I was visiting the area." He hoped he'd covered his embarrassment at having to lie.

"Ah, well, I have an aunt called Maggie, but she's not here. Of course, she isn't a Harrison now. Married for years to Uncle Alex, but he's dead. Lovely lady. Always busy. Your mother obviously didn't care too much when they were younger if she didn't keep in touch!"

"No, I suppose not. Probably just curious since I was passing through. I don't suppose you know where she ended up living?"

"Since she wouldn't know you, it doesn't really matter, does it? Still, it's the smallholding on the right as you go up the hill. Now, I must ask you to leave, as I have to walk the dog." With this dismissal, Ed strode towards the front door, leaving Bob staring into space.

With a last long glance at the exterior of the house, he made his way back to the car. Almost in a daze, he put the car into gear and slowly drove up the hill, stopping nervously at the curb before a five-bar gate that led into a cobbled yard. He climbed out of the car, his legs feeling numb, as if the blood couldn't reach them. He forced one foot in front of the other, walking up to the gate and peering into the yard. He heard voices, presumably coming from the house to the left, and he could see the land reaching back to a small copse. He didn't dare open the gate, so he dragged himself past the front of the house, trying to take in every detail of its flaking paint and tumbling garden walls. It looked as if it had seen better days, and Ed's comment that Sam was dead began to form some kind of impression of a struggle to keep the smallholding going. The fruit trees were almost bare, but they looked strong enough, and over the wall he could see a large raised bed that someone had obviously tended.

Bob's heart seemed to be beating at twice its normal rate, a sensation he hadn't felt since he'd been in a state of high alert in the navy. He wished someone would come out of one of the doors, so he might just glimpse one of the occupants—maybe even her.

He lingered at the end of the plot, looking around as if waiting for someone to find him guilty of loitering, but eventually he turned and walked back to the car, imagining the woman he might call "mother" somewhere behind those windows. He didn't dare knock. He could cause chaos, and he might not be welcome. Perhaps he would come back another day. At least he knew where she had lived. She had been real. She had been a wife, an aunt. A hunger he hadn't previously known gripped him. *What was she like?* He knew now that he'd opened this Pandora's box, it was never going to close.

Chapter Nine

1945

It was a beautiful morning; one of those days when the gentle English sun was at its Winter best, shining against a beautiful blue sky that cast a brilliant light on the wall of the bedroom. Maggie sang to herself as she forced the brush through her stubbornly curly hair, taming it into an attempt at tidy rolls. It wouldn't last—it never did. But she didn't mind. Nothing could suppress her smile and happiness that morning. The previous day had been bliss.

She'd been walking home with Bill when he stopped suddenly by the footpath at the end of the road. His arm whirled her round to behind the hedge, out of reach of streetlights and prying eyes. When he'd cupped her face in his hands, looked into her eyes, and told her she was beautiful, she knew she'd met the man of her dreams.

Maggie's lips moved towards his as if pulled by some invisible force, and she felt his passion ignite hers. When his hands travelled over her shoulders, she pressed herself against him, savouring his caress through the back of her dress. She'd never felt this stirring in her body before, and she knew she'd let him do whatever he wanted to do.

Bill reached round to the front of her dress, undid the buttons, and slid his hand over her breast, squeezing it slightly. She shuddered, as if she were cold, feeling she should pull away but knowing she wouldn't. When he reached under her skirt, she kissed him harder, felt his tongue explore her mouth, and her eyes closed with pleasure. As he fumbled with the buttons on his trousers, she tightened her arms around his neck, and suddenly she was lying on the cold grass, her coat stretched out beneath her.

Bill landed gently on top, moving into her. "I love you," he whispered into her hair. "I want to spend the rest of my life with you."

"I love you, too." Maggie could hardly believe she had said it. She never imagined this was how love was between a woman and a man, but right now all that mattered was this moment. Her first experience of this kind of love felt as if some miracle had happened, and she knew she would never be the same again.

Later, as Bill walked her home, his arm around her shoulders, she muttered, "I wish we didn't have to say goodbye. I wish we could spend more time together."

He kissed the top of her head. "I know. It's rotten luck that I can't be with you for Valentine's Day. Wherever I am, you know you'll be my Valentine. We just have to wait until my next pass. I'll see you as soon as I can."

Maggie now knew what it was to feel like a woman, and her heart told her she couldn't wait until they could repeat that passionate abandon.

She'd first met Bill quite by accident. She'd been riding her horse, Juno, round the quiet country lanes, when suddenly two idiots on bicycles had come laughing round a bend towards her, ringing their bells like children with new toys. Juno was startled, and she was almost propelled into the hedge at the side of the road. One of the men seemed oblivious, but she saw the face of the other change in an instant as he realised what was happening. Their eyes met—hers with an icy stare, his apologetic.

"Shut up, you fool," Bill flung at his companion. The laughter quelled, and the cyclists stopped as if glued to the spot. It was probably only seconds, but it felt like minutes to Maggie as she regained control and was able to carry on down the road.

The next time they saw each other was three months later, when she and her best friend, Rosemary, went to a dance in the town, knowing that some of the young airmen from the nearby base would be there, but not really expecting to do more than look at them from afar. Again, Bill caught her eye as he stood drinking and joking at the bar with a group of loud men. Obviously making the most of their chance to exploit the attraction of their youth and uniforms, some of them made coarse remarks as the girls passed, getting coy responses and some not-so-coy rebuffs. Bill turned towards her, making a feeble gesture of holding the reins of a horse, confirming recognition. Maggie nodded, then turned away—Rosemary desperate to know who he was.

"He's one of the maniacs that nearly had me unseated," explained Maggie. "One of those cyclists that shouldn't have been let loose on the world."

"Oh, he looks nice, though, Maggie."

"Hmm." Maggie walked to the other side of the room, Rosemary trailing after her.

They sat down, content to be wallflowers, watching the dancers as the music sprung up. Couples got to their feet, and the floor came alive with the energy of the jitterbug, everyone dancing as if there might not be a tomorrow. Suddenly, there he was in front of her, asking if she'd do him the honour of dancing with him. Taken aback by his politeness, Maggie was caught off guard and had to be nudged by Rosemary. Still, as she opened her mouth, nothing came out, and she found herself accepting with a nod, against her better judgement.

Annie Harrison secretly worried when a raven-haired young man in an air force uniform arrived on her doorstep and asked permission to take Maggie out during his forty-eight-hour pass. He seemed nice enough—shuffling awkwardly on the doorstep and clutching his cap in both hands—but she knew what heartache these war-time romances could bring. It didn't seem that long since her sister had lost the man she loved to the trenches of the Great War. They'd been so young, so full of hope that at least it had been the war to end all wars, a noble sacrifice. But that had been part of the great lie that had taken so many boyfriends, husbands, fathers, and beautiful young sons to their death.

It had not ended war. Here they were again, nearly thirty years later, when Annie was grateful that farming was a reserved occupation, and her husband was safely a vet in his fifties, not a fighter. When the news had come—"We are now at war with Germany"—she'd wanted to scream, "Not again. Not more mothers' tears for sons who don't come back!"

She'd listened to Churchill say, "We will fight them on the beaches," stirring the young into patriotic support, but her heart had sunk. They hadn't known much about what was happening on a distant battlefield of the Great War, but this time the radio fed them the news they craved, yet dreaded, and the bombs brought the war to them. She knew how many mothers of young pilots just wanted their sons back, and that medals would never fill the hole in their hearts.

It made no difference. Maggie had the bravery of youth and the determination that growing up turned into defiance. She would see her airman, with or without her mother's blessing. At least allowing Maggie to see him meant Annie knew who her daughter was with. While her mother worried, Maggie smiled and laughed while danger beckoned, as only those in love can. She refused to contemplate the possibility that war could wrench apart her dreams, following the insistent inward nagging that she must take the happiness while she could.

It was Annie who first noticed her daughter's smile was fading. She saw that Maggie had hardly touched her breakfast. At first, she thought it was because the airman hadn't been seen for a couple weeks, though this wasn't all that surprising. There was a feeling that something big was about to happen. The tide had turned against Hitler, the Americans were making progress, and they heard planes taking off and landing — a lot of activity at the airfield. Sometimes she found herself counting them out and counting them back, but lately she'd avoided that. Then, with a heart-wrenching realisation, she heard Maggie being sick in the outside privy.

Chapter Ten

1945

Maggie arrived at her Auntie Betty's in the middle of a cloudburst. The ride from the station underlined just how far she would be from all she knew. Ern, an elderly farm hand, had been sent to meet her with an old pony and cart that had both seen better days.

On her left hand, she wore the curtain ring that was to serve as her wedding ring for the next few months. She clutched her battered brown case as the cart bumped its way up the winding, climbing lanes, passing lush pastures in farm after farm full of strangers. By the time they reached what looked like a large estate on the left, everything was dripping—the cart, the driver, the horse, and Maggie, with puddles forming at her feet. She no longer really cared. As the lane narrowed, and the stone walls closed in, her sense of inescapable fate overwhelmed her. How could this be happening to her? Six weeks ago, she'd been extremely happy. She knew she'd found her soul mate, and she knew she would love him for the rest of her life. When he told her he loved her, she'd known that her mother would say she was throwing her life away on a dream, but she had gone beyond dreaming. This was real. When the war was over, they were going to marry. They couldn't get an engagement ring, but they'd made their pledge to each other.

And now... now she knew nothing anymore. Bill hadn't been near her since that day, and there'd been no messages. Maggie tried to go to the base, but there was no way she could get past the guards. It was only when she spotted one of the other airmen in the village that she managed to find out anything. He hadn't looked her in the face when she asked why Bill had not been in contact, he had just said, "Sorry. He didn't make it back from Dresden. So sorry..." and rushed away, leaving her clutching her purse so tightly her fingers had gone white.

Instantly, the world had become distant—sound irrelevant as she felt the blood drain from her face. She'd sat down on the old wooden seat by the phone box, staring into a distance her eyes weren't really seeing. Somehow, she'd walked home, but she had no recollection of getting there.

Maggie's mother was chopping vegetables as she came through the back door, but a casual glance at her daughter, and the knife dropped to the draining board with a clatter. She'd seen that look before—on her sister, her aunt, and so many others. She folded a rigid Maggie into her arms, talking into her ear until she finally made contact with the shell her daughter had become. Maggie's shoulders relaxed as her body crumpled into her mother's chest, and the sobs came.

From that moment, Maggie's world fell apart, and she became an automaton, functioning without feeling, because feeling was too painful, too frightening, too unbearable.

Auntie Betty was a kindly soul who told her neighbours her niece's husband had been a brave young pilot—fighting to his death in a raid. Asking no questions, her neighbours made sympathetic, admiring noises to her face. Maggie nodded and said *hello* as she passed them huddled on corners, baskets on their arms, sideways glances telling their own tale of what they believed this sinful girl had done. She felt them look her up and down, knowing, judging, polite but distant.

She carried her guilt in every step. Time stood still in Maggie's mind, but her child insisted that it passed. She focused on her daily routine, ignoring her changing shape and refusing to think about what would happen when the baby came. The gossips got used to her being around, and she sensed a shift in their interest. She'd arrived in spring, and already there were rumblings of Hitler losing the war. The chatter in the village began to ignore her as the air filled with a tense hope, as fragile as moth's wings, that soon their days of rationing and fear might just be coming to an end.

The radio became essential listening, as each day the news became more vital. In Betty's little cottage, as across the valleys and the hills, a cheer went up when the news came through that Hitler had committed suicide. Newspaper headlines revelled in the event, the Daily Express declaring that "Germans put out the news everyone hopes is true". At last, there was an optimism no one had felt for such a long time. The surrender was signed. Union Jacks began to appear everywhere, and then, at three o'clock on 7th May, never to be forgotten by Maggie's generation, came the news flash they'd waited for. The BBC announced that Victory in Europe Day would be a national holiday to take place the following day. Special editions of the newspapers appeared, passed excitedly around households. A huge bonfire was lit on the hill behind the shops, and bunting was going up all over the village. Betty's gnarled, arthritic fingers laced themselves around Maggie's smooth hand, her gentle silence a comforting acknowledgement of joy and sadness woven into the tapestry of the day.

Mothers started organising a street party for the children whose fathers might now come home and see them grow up. The church bells rang, summoning everyone to a thanksgiving service that very evening; it didn't matter that it wasn't Sunday. The school children made hats and flags. Betty and Maggie watched proudly from the doorstep, as the church choir led a parade along the high street and round the village green.

Thousands of people had headed for London. Here, people had been together through thick and thin. They knew each other's missing men and comforted each other's children while the planes flew overhead to who-knew-where. It was enough that they stood together in celebration and relief and triumph. Churchill warned that victory in Japan was still to come, so rejoicing would be brief, but rejoice they would.

Maggie wondered what it would be like to be one of those women singing as they gathered tables and chairs in the street. She watched the children eating and drinking and having fun, and even she had to feel the stirrings of something others would call joy. A wan smile lit up her face, and she joined in as they ended the party with the national anthem, standing alongside old Mr Evans, who dressed in his Home Guard uniform for the occasion and solemnly saluted those he would never see again.

King George gave a radio broadcast, praising the people's endurance and calling for lasting peace—paying tribute to those who couldn't join in any celebrations. Maggie's eyes filled with silent tears, her hand flying to her stomach as he said: "Let us remember those who will not come back...let us remember the men in all the services, and the women in all the services, who have laid down their lives. We have come to the end of our tribulation, and they are not with us at the moment of rejoicing."

Maggie would remember. She would remember forever.

In August, Japan's surrender came. Prime Minister Clement Atlee confirmed the news in a broadcast, saying: "The last of our enemies is laid low," and then he thanked the allies.

It was again the king whose broadcast spoke to Maggie: "Our hearts are full to overflowing, as are your own. Yet there is not one of us who has experienced this terrible war who does not realise that we shall feel its inevitable consequences long after we have all forgotten our rejoicings today."

Little did he know just how long she would live with the consequences.

Betty pinned up her silver hair and pulled on her clean, starched pinafore every morning, but she'd begun to rely on Maggie to do the things her old body rebelled against, like scrubbing and cleaning. It was now becoming difficult for Maggie to whiten the doorstep or turn the mangle while the baby protested with kicks under her ribs. As autumn began to bite, she swept up the leaves that floated down from the trees on the hillside above the cottages, piling them into the compost heap at the end of the garden—once full of vegetables her uncle had grown, but now neglected and weary. While her aunt continued to cook, she went back and forth to the village shop, her coat no longer covering her shame.

At the end of October, Maggie was carrying in another bucket of coal to light the kitchen fire when she felt a strange fluttering. She clenched her teeth with a determination to carry on, hitching the bucket higher on her hip. Silhouetted against the rays of a rusty-orange sunrise, she held on to the numbness she'd clung to since arriving on the farm. Her scarf-clad head bowed against the wind as she trudged around the yard in her heavy boots, willing her feet to move. She raised her blank eyes to the sky, as if chiding a god who had deserted her, before turning back towards the enfolding darkness of the house.

Maggie tried to ignore the tightening and crumpled up the newspaper, carefully setting the kindling sticks on top before she found the flint. As she knelt in front of the grate, it happened again, this time stronger, taking her breath away with surprise. She struck the flint and caught the paper, throwing on coal as the flames wove their way through the sticks.

She heard the creak of the bed springs, signalling that Auntie Betty would be up soon, waiting until there was some welcoming warmth downstairs. Maggie filled the old, black kettle and set it to boil on the range. Before she could make the tea, another contraction bent her forward, and she knew something was happening. No one had told her what to expect, and Auntie Betty had never carried a pregnancy to full term. But Betty had lived among the women of the village all her life, and as she came through the kitchen door and looked on the scene—Maggie clutching her stomach and leaning on the sink, the floor wet beneath her—it told her enough. As if an actress in a speeded-up film, Maggie was swept into a chair.

"Maggie, your labour's started. I'm going to get help." Grabbing her coat, Betty was suddenly wide awake.

Walking faster than she'd been able to in recent months, she made her way to the farmhouse at the end of the lane. She hammered on the back door, shouting at the same time, "Aggie! Aggie, come quick! It's our Maggie! It's started!"

Aggie appeared at the door, headscarf tied round her head, the smell of bacon wafting past her. She pulled on her mac as they started back down the hill. As a farmer's wife, birth and death were no strangers to her, and many a young woman had been to her door, trusting that she would know what to do.

They reached the cottage as Maggie was doubling up and screaming, terrified by what her body was doing to her. Aggie immediately took control, sending Betty to get the bed ready while she worked out how close Maggie was to giving birth.

"Right, young lady. Let's get you sorted out," Aggie said, sensing that Maggie had no idea what to do.

Five minutes and two contractions later, Maggie was in her nightgown on her bed. As day broke, she began pushing without any choice. She shouted and screamed until Aggie interrupted, "Put your energy into getting this baby born, because it's getting impatient! Come on, girl. Give it all you've got! I can see the head!"

Maggie thought her body would rip in two as she gave birth to the head, and then came more, as she pushed the rest of the body into the world.

A church-like hush hung over the room, and the women were moving briskly round the bed. Exhausted, Maggie saw Aggie pick up the baby by its feet and slap its bottom, hard. A yell filled the room, and Aggie and Betty smiled at each other across the foot of the bed.

Maggie abruptly found the baby on her chest, and as her hands moved themselves to steady him, she watched his skin slowly turn from blue to pink, as he cried. She felt her body contract one more time, and she was aware that Aggie was sorting something out, but all she could focus on was the miracle of what her bump had become—this squalling, writhing human being that was her son.

Confined to her lying-in for the next few days, Maggie learned to feed her son by Aggie placing the baby forcefully on her breast, then standing over her. The new mother talked to him, sang to him, changed his nappies, and learnt to recognise the way he screwed up his brow before he cried. She found he stopped crying when she held and rocked him, and despite herself, she began to love him. Wherever he was, she knew an invisible bond, like a delicate chiffon scarf, would always wrap itself around her heart. When they asked her for a name, she called him Richard, after her grandfather. It was a safe name.

Six weeks after the birth, Maggie was to return to her parents on the condition that she did not come home with the baby. It had all been arranged. When Richard was five weeks old, a knock at the door heralded the arrival of a Mrs Smith, a bustling middle-aged woman, who came to look at Richard and Auntie Betty while Maggie was despatched to the farmyard to avoid any emotional outburst. It was left to Betty to hold Maggie against her strong shoulder as she broke the news that Mrs Smith would be back in three days to collect the baby and his things. Maggie had no idea where he was going, but she was told she could write a letter which would be kept on his file. She carefully gathered the few clothes she and her aunt had managed to knit for him and those given as presents by some of the villagers, and she tied a ribbon round the letter, praying that it carried with it something of the tenderness with which she wrote. She was to hand over the baby outside the cottage, and then to go straight back into the kitchen. It was all very matter of fact, as if he were a Christmas parcel being collected. She didn't dare let herself feel until it was done, and Mrs Smith was driven away in a shining black Morris Minor, holding Richard as stiffly as she wore her hat.

Maggie was torpefied, her eyes clouded with tears she was holding back. She ran towards the farm where she could hide in the cow byre, and then she sobbed. Her body shook as if it were in labour all over again, her knees giving way beneath her as she sank into a bale of hay, trying to stifle the noise with her gloves, for fear of being discovered. She cried until exhaustion left her with no more tears that day, and she made her way back to the cottage. Betty watched her make her way to her bedroom where the empty drawer they'd used as a cradle was the only evidence that Richard had been part of their lives.

The following day, Maggie packed her case and made her way back to her parents in a blur of grief. Her parting from her aunt had seemed to seal the finality of the surrender. Betty put her arms around the girl she had become inordinately fond of, feeling that Maggie was like the daughter she might have had, if her babies had lived.

"Maggie, my love," Betty began. "Oh Maggie! You take care of yourself now! I shall miss you, my girl. I certainly will. You're a good girl. You just remember that your love for that little baby will last as long as the coal in these mountains, just as mine has for my babies that didn't stay. You did right by him. He'll have a good future because you've given him the best start you can. And if ever you want to come back to see your old auntie, you know there will always be an open door for you, girl." Her voice broke as she kissed Maggie on the top of her head and almost pushed her away. "Go on now, girl, or you'll miss your train. Your mam will be waiting for you. You're her child, and she'll have missed you."

Not daring to speak, Maggie climbed aboard the cart that had brought her here all those weeks ago. This time, the sun shone weakly through the branches, almost as if smiled, pleased that she felt such desolation. As she climbed down with her battered case, old Ern lifted his cap and muttered a brief, "Safe journey miss." He was gone as soon as her second foot touched the ground, and she felt as alone as she had the day she first left home.

She imagined everyone on the train somehow knew her secret as she pulled her hat down a little further than was fashionable, hoping to avoid catching anyone's eye. She was relieved to find a vacant window seat where she could stare out across the landscape or lean against the pane, eyes closed, trying not to think. With so many women coping with so much in those early days of peace, she hoped that no one would ask her why she mopped the silent tears that escaped from the corners of her eyes.

She clutched her coat across her empty womb and studied the houses and farms where others' shattered lives were played out in her head as she sped past them. She imagined the widows, the orphans, the mothers and fathers who suffered the loss of war, and she wondered how they dealt with this feeling that someone had taken her insides in two hands and wrung them out in the mangle, leaving them knotted and crushed.

There was no one to meet Maggie when she finally arrived. As she got off the train, she looked around at the old, familiar station. It had always been there, and she'd never noticed much about it, but suddenly it was as if she'd landed somewhere completely different. The paint peeling from the nearby posts reflected her feeling that everyone could see below her outward appearance. Just as the rust had been poorly hidden by the black coating of paint, her secret could easily be revealed.

The porter was busy at the other end of the train, off-loading parcels and mail. Maggie was able to slip through the entrance with her case, avoiding any offer to carry it, which might have led to a question about where she had been, and why. She looked straight ahead as she took her first determined step on the road back to the village. It was a road she'd travelled countless times, but now the tarmac seemed to dare her to walk as if she belonged, after falling so far from grace. She welcomed the descending darkness, hiding her face and her shame as she approached her parents' house. With no sign of anyone waiting at the gate, she made her way round to the back door and let herself in.

The kitchen was scented with roasting meat and potatoes, steam clinging to the windows, resisting escape through the open vent. Her mother turned towards her, a worried frown the only outward sign of welcome.

"Hello, Mum," was all Maggie could manage to say.

Annie wiped her hands on her apron, seemingly in control, then threw her arms open and ran across the kitchen. She grasped her daughter with relief that she was safe again and wrapped one hand around the back of Maggie's head, holding it to her. She uttered nothing but told all through the comfort of a mother's love.

As quickly as she'd embraced Maggie, she pulled away, straightened herself, and said, "Your father is out at the Western Farm, but he'll be home soon. Take your case upstairs and get yourself ready for dinner. It'll be on the table in half an hour."

It was as if Maggie had just been out for the day. She understood the unspoken message. They would clear away any sign that she'd been away. Normal behaviour was to be established as soon as possible. There was to be no talk of what had happened or how she felt. The episode was at an end, and she must now revert to being the daughter she was before this interruption to their routine.

Maggie would cry forever for Richard, at first loudly and daily. Gradually she was able to keep the display less visible, but she was always weeping on the inside—especially when his birthday came around in the autumn, when she would often be seen taking long walks down the road and up the footpath. On the surface, she returned to her respectable life, with her respectable parents, and no one mentioned the events of that year again. She could often feel her mother's eyes following her, saying more than she would ever venture to express, but her father retreated behind his newspaper when he came in from work, and conversation was sparse. He said nothing, and there were no recriminations, but her whole body felt the chasm between them now that his little girl had flown too close to the sun. Maggie's brother was rarely in the house, and she didn't dare confide in any of her friends. Like a thick coat of insulation, silence fell to protect the family from the shame and scandal, locking it away in the past, so that it no longer existed for anyone but Maggie. If her mother wondered about her grandchild, only her eyes betrayed her.

PART THREE

"The past is always with us, for nothing that once was time can ever depart"

- Rabindrabanath Tragore (First non-European to be awarded the Nobel Prize for Literature - 1913)

CHAPTER 11

1950

It had been a long, wet day, but the evening was a forgiving one. The sun was just beginning to set across the distant hill, bathing grazing sheep in an orange glow, setting the stubby grass on fire, despite the cold. Gold, red, and navy-blue clouds mingled as if painted by numbers, reminiscent of a jigsaw puzzle Maggie could remember piecing together one soggy afternoon. She stood at the conservatory door in awe at the spectacle of beauty. The willow tree at the end of the garden was bursting into leaf, and primulas graced the edges of her father's neatly tended beds. She took a deep breath, soaking up the promise of new life all around her. Time had passed in a haze of grief and loss and the suppression of both.

Maggie continued smiling at neighbours who welcomed her home, pretending to have enjoyed her stay with her auntie. She did her best not to notice babies in prams, which seemed to be all around her. Whenever she could, she would sneak away to her room, where at least she had the freedom to think her own thoughts, even if they often left her exhausted and blotched with tears. She had one photograph of her tiny son, and she held it close as she talked to him. Her parents hadn't seen it or asked about him—blocked him out of their future.

Since the day she came back from the station, Maggie's father held her in his arms as if welcoming a stranger, and nothing of what had happened was mentioned in the house. He took up his place in his favourite armchair at the end of the day, as he always did, and her mother bustled around her, putting on the kettle and feeding the dogs.

She felt trapped in this pretend life, suffocated by the routine normality, when she wanted to scream that she had a son and needed to see him.

She'd brought home one tiny matinee jacket that she knitted herself, and a pair of bootees her aunt had made. She held them to her nose, smelling his scent, as fragrant to her as a bouquet of flowers. She felt like a shattered vase that would never hold that precious aroma again. She placed the jacket carefully back in the box and returned it to its banishment in the bottom of the wardrobe.

Slowly, gradually, Maggie settled back into the old patterns of life. Much against her father's wishes, she took a job in the local post office and store. There the widowed Olive Randall had been struggling on without her Wilf, who hadn't come back from North Africa. Olive was a kindly soul and recognised Maggie as someone who knew about loss—assuming it was the loss of her pilot. Together they travelled the road so many trod, saying nothing about how they felt but each of them somehow sensing the support of the other, drawing strength from a shared smile and busying themselves with orders and customers who talked about ordinary, everyday things.

When Olive scurried back and forth between her children going to school or coming home or needing food, she was grateful for someone who asked no questions but instinctively knew when to deflect a customer straying into chatter about a lazy husband or wishing they had never married.

The couple had known only a few years of happiness, and how Olive wished Wilf would walk through the door, lift her off her feet and grin at her as he asked if his dinner was ready. Three children had been the result of their love, each one being welcomed as a sign of them growing a family of their own and nights the like of which she would never know again. She missed Wilf's touch, his snoring in her ear, his wicked laugh when he tickled her, his silly jokes when he'd had a beer too many, his gentle love. He'd held the youngest in his arms the day he went away, kissing him on his forehead and promising to take him to a football match as soon as he was old enough. Ted would never remember that, as he was only two, but Olive would forever be sad that he didn't keep his promise.

Fred had sat on his father's knee and thought his uniform exciting as he played with the button, and Wilf let him try on his cap. His four-year-old self believed his dad was going on a great adventure, and his eyes shone with pride.

Dick, the eldest, wore a worried frown. He didn't understand about war yet, but at school people talked in whispers about fighting and death, and although he didn't understand it, he knew death was horrible, and you didn't come back from it. They'd buried the cat in the garden, and he was afraid of his dad's adventure ending that way. He didn't cry, because he was the big boy, and his dad told him he would have to be the man of the family, but he wished he could rush at his mum's apron, so she would wrap her arms round him and tell him it would all be all right. He wanted it to be all right.

Maggie watched the boys grow, wondering where her son was and what he was like now. She imagined him playing with other boys, his smile like hers, his eyes shining with excitement. She hoped, desperately, that he was happy wherever he was.

She'd been making a delivery to the big house when she met Sam. He was on his knees in front of the rose beds as she approached the front door, obviously not expecting anyone to call. His spade had fallen over, and it and a trug full of tiny nettles and thistles blocked the path.

As he spotted her walking towards the pile of weeds, he jumped up. "Oh, sorry miss," Sam said. "Let me move these out of the way."

"Thank you," was all she managed to say as she took in his tanned face and imposing frame.

As he doffed his cap, a shock of strawberry-blonde hair tumbled down over his eyes, almost as blue as hers. He pushed it back with large, strong hands stained by earth. His shirt sleeves were rolled up, and braces held his old corduroy trousers in place as he bent around the plants. A large scar on his left arm suggested he had not been unscathed in the war, but nevertheless he looked content and confident, as he said, "We haven't met before, have we? I'm Sam Mitchell. I'm the new estate manager, but at the moment I seem to be mostly managing myself, as we still haven't got enough staff. Sorry—can't shake your hand..." His lop-sided smile met Maggie's serious face, and she found herself liking this man, despite herself. She responded to his warmth with a smile that crept from her mouth to her eyes, and she hoped she'd meet him again.

Meet him again she did, as he became a customer, one she was pleased to see coming through the door. When he asked her to go with him to the village fete, she couldn't refuse, and so began his courting. Her heart still ached for her lost love, but in Sam she found comfort and a friend. It was easy to accept when he asked her to become his wife on New Year's Eve, as they celebrated the beginning of a new decade. There was still rationing, but the end of the war-time austerity was in sight, and they felt a surge of hope as the clock struck midnight.

Sam got down on his knees and produced a curtain ring, which made Maggie laugh outwardly but shrink inwardly, and she allowed him to joke as she put it on her finger. As she stared at the ring, remembering the last time she'd worn one, Sam shouted above the noise of Perry Como coming from the gramophone in the corner. "A—you're adorable," he sang at the top of his voice. "Marry me!"

She nodded, and he kissed her as if tomorrow might never come. Maggie fought her memory, accepting Sam's passion as a chance of happiness she thought would never come, but still the sadness stalked her somewhere in her stomach and her brain, calling her a traitor to her past love.

"Oh, Maggie, that's wonderful!" beamed her mother when Maggie broke the news of her engagement. "Your father will be so pleased!"

Maggie saw the relief in her mother's face that she was going to join the ranks of the respectable women of the village, sealing up her indiscretion and confining it to her unacknowledged past. Sam met their expectations of eligible, respectable young men, and his handsome face had won her mother over from the first time she met him.

Her father had never quite forgiven Maggie for the shadow she cast on the family name. He seemed to know that gossip had smeared their reputation, and reputation was something he treasured—his family line stretching back through generations of holding status in the locality. As a vet, he relied on his clientele respecting him, and Maggie knew she'd let him down badly. He'd been a good husband and father, a provider who worked long hours and expected his wife's role to be the homemaker and the one who brought up the children. His relationship with Maggie and her brother had been a distant presence, and they were wary of his discipline, knowing that children should be seen and not heard in his company. He'd become more distant from Maggie in the last few years, though he'd forged some kind of bond with his son, with whom he could go shooting or fishing on school holidays, grooming him to follow in his footsteps.

To others, Maggie's father seemed to beam with pride as he led his daughter into the little church where villagers lined the pathway to the old wooden porch. She floated up the aisle in her long, full-skirted dress lined with petticoats to ensure that no one could stand within a foot of her without crushing it. She clutched her bouquet in one hand, her father's arm in the other, desperately trying to blot out thoughts of virginal white, like an enveloping lie, betraying her past. She fought her memory, focusing on the tears of happiness on her mother's face and the anxious waiting of the man who had brought her back from despair.

She'd given Sam the chance to run when she told him about her first love. Instead, he'd taken her face in his hands and kissed her forehead. He'd been in love before and told her, "There but for the grace of God went my first girl." Maggie understood the girl he'd loved before the war could easily have ended up in the same predicament as she did—pregnant and alone. They'd feared there wasn't much time to live, or to love, when Sam had been called up. His first love married a fireman while he was away fighting, and he hadn't heard from her again. He had heard, through a mutual friend, that she'd given birth to a daughter shortly after her marriage, and to this day, he didn't know whether or not she'd carried his child.

Sam didn't have Maggie's certainty of loss, but the bond of understanding strengthened, rather than weakened, their love for each other and their determination to have a child of their own as soon as possible.

Life, of course, had other ideas. Maggie gave up her job to become a housewife and hopefully a mother. Months slipped past, turning into more than a year, and she was beginning to give up hope, when suddenly, one morning not long after Christmas, she felt again that sickness that could only be one thing. She could hardly contain her excitement when Sam came in from work, focused on cleaning himself up and wanting his meal.

"I'm sorry it's late," Maggie managed to say, the smell of the greens she boiled filling her with overwhelming nausea. "You see, I've been feeling a bit sick..."

At first, Sam continued washing his hands in the sink, splashing soil up the sides as if someone had tipped mud all over its white surface. He turned to grab a towel from the rack by the cooker and took a sideways glance at Maggie. "You don't look too good, actually. Are you OK? Do you need to see the doctor?"

"I need to see the doctor soon, Sam," Maggie replied. "But I'm not ill, just feeling sick."

Sam almost backed into the table as the possibility dawned on him. Then a huge grin spread across his face, and Maggie was reminded of that day they first met.

Chapter Twelve

1952

Maggie had her first miscarriage the day the king died. It was a cold February day when she recognised the pain she had felt that day in her aunt's yard. She hoped she was wrong, and it was just a stomach upset.

Sam was at the Hall tending the seedlings he hoped would provide a blaze of colour in a few months' time. Despite the size of the house and the estate, he found himself a jack-of-all-trades, including gardening. The wealth of the Smyth-Richardsons had dwindled since the war, and the young men drifted off to the towns and factories for better jobs and better pay.

Maggie knew she would not make it to the phone box at the end of the road, and Sam wasn't due home for another two hours. She gripped the back of the chair, the door handle, the old mangle outside the back door. She made her way to the toilet where a rush of blood confirmed her fears. Too scared to cry, she knew that as she pulled the chain on the old cistern, there was a tiny fragment of life disappearing before her eyes. As the nation mourned the loss of the king, it felt as if it were mourning for her, too.

Perhaps this is my punishment for giving away my son, she thought. *Maybe I haven't been careful enough, or I'm just not good enough to be a mother...* Perhaps she was not worthy of another pregnancy. *I deserve this*. Her head spun.

When Sam arrived home, he found her on the sofa, tears dried on her blotched, sleeping face and her clothes bearing testimony to the truth she wouldn't have to tell him. He stared around the room and felt the gulp in the back of his throat. He crept out to the scullery where he could weep without waking her, before heading to his brother's house a few streets away.

"Sam, what's up?" Phillip asked from the doorway as he scanned his brother's drawn, pale face.

"It's Maggie, Phil. I think she's lost the baby." Sam rubbed his fingers across his forehead, as though trying to make sense of what he'd seen.

From behind them, Penny appeared. "Where is she?"

"She's asleep on the sofa, Pen. I don't know what to do. How could it happen? How can I possibly make this better?" His shoulders heaved in helpless despair.

By the time Sam had finished talking, Penny had grabbed her coat from the hook in the hall and was on her way through the front door.

"I'll be back later, Phil." Turning to Sam, Penny said, "You can't leave her on her own! What if she wakes up and you're not there? You stay here with Phil. Have a drink. It's about all you're good for at the moment! Leave Maggie to me, though God knows seeing me this size won't help much." She tapped her stomach where her baby kicked against her hand.

Men, Penny thought. *Useless at a time like this.* She quickened her steps, knowing that her sister-in-law needed the comfort of a woman who would understand just what she was going through.

By the time Maggie woke, there was a steaming pot of tea, a stew on the stove, and a warm pair of arms to wrap around her. She exhausted her body with crying before climbing into bed alone.

It was not long afterwards that Olive Randall came to their door asking for help. Teddy hadn't been feeling well, and the doctor had delivered the news every parent dreaded: polio. Its curse had been rearing its head in other areas of the country, and a girl called Minnie had been sick in the school playground. Teddy had suddenly become weak and feverish, and Olive thought he was coming down with the flu, but then he complained of a stiff neck and pain in his legs. When the doctor came out to see him, he immediately ordered an ambulance. Teddy had been driven off to the isolation hospital on the outskirts of the nearby town.

"Maggie," Olive began. "Oh Maggie, I didn't know where to turn! I need to visit our Teddy, but there are the other children. No one with children of their own will take them because they're all so afraid. Would you be able to look after them for a few hours?" She was sobbing by the time she finished. She knew she wouldn't be able to hug her poor Teddy, and she would only be allowed in to see him for a short time, dressed in a gown and mask. She couldn't bear to think of him there, all on his own, frightened. She was terrified for him. She knew some people had ended up unable to breathe on their own and been confined to an iron lung. She knew Johnnie, up the road, was left in callipers and a huge shoe to make up the difference in the length of his legs. What was going to happen to her precious child?

Maggie fought the feeling of being punched in the stomach at the reference to her having no children, but Olive had been so good to her when she really needed a friend, and she could not turn her back.

"Of course, bring them here," Maggie said, praying at the same time that she wasn't putting herself and Sam at risk. The spectre of polio was something she hoped she would never see here, but she'd heard that it struck on both sides of the Atlantic, and it seemed to hit the children.

Maggie was very fond of Olive's children, and she found an outlet for her maternal instincts over the next months as she became Olive's salvation. Fortunately, and strangely, none of the others fell victim to what had hit their brother, and Teddy survived. Olive found the courage to carry on with the loss of her husband, and again Maggie saw her dig deep, focusing on keeping her little family together and fed. Her visits to Teddy left her drained and distraught, as he cried to be cuddled, and she said she felt like a monster for not being able to. On the bus ride back home, Olive allowed herself a few minutes to give way to her own fears and thoughts, but the moment she was greeted by her other children, she was bustling and brave, her wartime spirit carrying her through.

It was a joyful day when Teddy finally came out of hospital and into his mother's arms. His limp didn't stop him from joining the other children playing in the street, and Olive and Maggie were relieved that he hadn't been paralysed, as so many had in America that year.

When the children stopped needing Maggie to look after them, the old yearning returned, and Maggie wept with joy for Olive and sadness for herself, seeming never to be able to know that overwhelming mother's love.

It seemed to be a year determined to test them to their limit. Maggie had ignored what was happening to her body while she was so focused on Olive's children, and by the time the familiar sickness took a hold, she realised she was already six weeks pregnant. She was almost afraid to tell Sam in case she was to disappoint him once again, but she knew she wouldn't be able to hide it for long.

They were once more full of hope, quietly listening to "The Navy Lark" on their new Bakelite radio when there was an urgent knock on the front door. Sam got up, sighing, wondering who was disturbing them. He took his time getting to the door and opened it slowly, ready to encourage whoever was on the other side to go away quickly. What he didn't expect was to be confronted by a policeman on his doorstep.

"Good evening, sir. Are you Mr Samuel Mitchell?"

"I am indeed, constable. What can I do for you?"

"May I come in, sir?" The seriousness in the officer's eyes was sobering. "I need to have a quiet word."

"Oh—yes, I suppose so. Come in. Come in." Sam led the way into the living—room where Maggie could hardly contain her amazement.

"I'm so sorry to disturb you, Mr Mitchell, Mrs Mitchell, but I'm afraid I have some unwelcome news. Mr Mitchell, are you the brother of Mr Phillip Mitchell of number two Gardenia Avenue?"

"Yes, I am, constable." Sam stiffened. "What's wrong? Is Phil in trouble?"

"I am afraid to tell you, sir, that Mr Phillip Mitchell was involved in an accident, and he suffered a fatal head injury."

Sam took a moment to process what he'd been told. He coughed into his hand as he struggled to work out the significance of "fatal". "Are you saying my brother is dead? He can't be. I saw him yesterday. He's only twenty-eight. He can't be dead..." Sam sank down onto the rocking chair with such force that it rocked back and forth, almost catapulting him out again. He stared ahead, seeing nothing.

The constable dipped his head in sympathy. "I'm sorry, sir, but they were crossing the road earlier today when a car backfired and startled a carthorse. The driver did his best to get it back under control, but he couldn't slow it down in time. Mr Mitchell managed to push the pram out of the way, but your brother was knocked down by the horse and caught by the cart's wheels. The ambulance crew tried to save him, but it wasn't possible."

"The baby—where's the baby? She's only a couple of months old!" asked Maggie, registering the pram, while Sam could only think of his brother.

"The baby is fine, madam. She's been taken to the hospital, but she'll have to go to the authorities tomorrow, so that someone can take care of her. I understand that the mother is already deceased, but the grandparents are on their way."

Sam couldn't process what he'd been told, and he couldn't respond with anything more than a shrug. They'd all been devastated when Penny lost her life in childbirth, but the poor child was now an orphan and Sam was the only close kin the police could trace in the immediate area.

"You said grandparents, constable. It can't be Phil's parents, so how did you find Penny's parents?" Maggie asked. "She was estranged from them." *Why weren't we the first to know?*

"It seems the authorities had their names on record, Mrs Mitchell, because they were concerned about how the baby would be cared for when their daughter died. I'm afraid that's all I know."

Maggie instinctually wanted to bring the baby home but acknowledged she couldn't be the perfect substitute mother to one baby when her own was to arrive so soon. She and Penny recently had big plans to share their time with their babies, taking them out and enjoying seeing them play together. Amid the shock that was rocking Maggie and Sam's world, Penny's baby was to be gathered up by her parents to be taken south to live with them. She wasn't even christened yet. Phil was going to arrange it.

The grandparents travelled through the night to the hospital that was caring for their daughter's child, and by the time their son-in-law was buried, they had disappeared back to their own home. At the funeral, they promised to keep in touch with Sam and Maggie, but the letters never arrived.

Maggie lost her baby in the new year. Sam had insisted that she rest at the beginning of her pregnancy, and she'd been confined to the house, or to sitting in the garden all that summer, reading books and taking up the embroidery she hadn't done since she was a girl. The boredom made months seem like years, but she told herself it would all be worth it eventually.

Maggie woke Sam in the middle of the night when she felt the pain, clutching her belly and trembling. They didn't own a car yet, so he had to leave her while he ran to the phone box to call for an ambulance. Minutes crawled by like hours before she was loaded through the white doors and disappeared behind the dark windows. Neighbours peered round curtains as its bell clanged, but the ambulance crew could only comfort Maggie and deliver the tiny scrap of a girl as they hurtled through deserted streets. It was such a dark night that perhaps even the stars and moon couldn't bear to look.

Baby Lydia lived for three days. In her body no bigger than a pair of forceps, her tiny lungs struggled. She slipped away in the incubator, and the record of her brief life declared only that she was born and died.

Grief clasped Maggie and Sam like a bindweed wrapping itself around them, growing into every fibre of their being. Sam went to work, but he could find no pleasure in what he did. He didn't want to be with other people because their sympathy made it harder not to hold the tide of emotion below the surface. Others noticed that he may lift his cap to say good morning, but his smile was no longer in his eyes.

Once out of hospital, Maggie hid inside the house until she could no longer pretend she didn't need to shop. She felt the eyes following her in the street and heard the whispers as she passed, just as they had when she arrived at her aunt's. Scandal or tragedy, the gossips didn't know what to say to someone's face, so they consoled themselves with comments behind their righteous poses, crossing the street and silencing themselves when she came within earshot.

Faces looked full of sympathy, but what could she say when the butcher asked if she was feeling better? It was easier to say, "Yes, thank you. Much better," than to tell him she lay awake at night dreaming of a white coffin as big as a bread bin, seeing it disappear into the ground and knowing she would never hold her daughter in her arms. She couldn't tell the baker she thought she would die, that so much loss was more than she could bear, or that she knew she would never be better now.

She went about shopping and chores to fill her empty days. She and Sam stopped talking about anything other than the mundane because each of them preserved the fragile wall they built around their pain, and to allow a chink in it would be to risk the flood bursting through. In the night, they sought each other in comfort, rather than love, silence filling the space between them. They could cope with no more loss now, the wounds gaping so wide inside them that a silent pact ensured there would be no more pregnancies.

"They've bought a television up at the Hall, and the staff have been invited to watch the coronation next Tuesday," announced Sam at the end of May in 1953. Maggie could hear the excitement in his voice.

"Oh, that's wonderful, Sam! I heard they're going to televise it. No one's ever been able to sit at home and watch a coronation before, have they? Imagine that! Mrs Cuthbert's son's rented a set, and the whole family are going to squash into her front room to watch the ceremony. I wouldn't be surprised if half the street tries to cram in! I just hope it doesn't rain! We've got such plans!"

Maggie was full of admiration for the young queen. They were born in the same year, and she couldn't imagine how it must have felt to take on so much responsibility, or to tell her own government she was going to share her big day with her subjects, whatever they said.

The second morning of June dawned without the longed-for sunshine.

"Oh, dear me no! Not today! How can it be so windy and cold? And it looks like rain over the hills!" Maggie groaned, but she was determined nothing was going to spoil today for the village. She hurriedly dressed and made her way to Olive.

"The children are so excited!" beamed Olive. "They've got their fancy dress all ready. Come and have a look!"

Like all the other mothers in the village, Olive had created capes and hats from old curtains and even fourteen-year-old Dick joined in the merriment.

"Nearly a man, isn't he?" Olive commented, as Maggie felt a lump come to her throat at the sight of him dressed as a soldier.

"Come on then, Olive. We'd better get the tables set. Maybe the rain will hold off for us. I could hear the clatter of the chairs and tables just after dawn, so I know the men've put the furniture out for us." She grabbed her bag full of bunting, looped her arm through Olive's, and set off for the main road, leaving Dick to get the others to the school. Relieved to see the road blocked off to traffic, her spirits lifted at the sound of the chatter of the other women gathering.

"Edie!" Maggie called across the road. "Is there anyone at the school to round up the children? Have we got the fancy dress competition under way?"

"Don't worry, Maggie. All sorted," was the reply. "Lil and Joe are over there. They'll wait till we're ready to let them loose. I think we're going to freeze unless this wind drops!" Edie disappeared into the village hall kitchen armed with a tray of sandwiches in each hand. The smell of baking wafted out through the open doors; every housewife had been up half the night baking their cakes of all shapes and sizes.

The trestle tables were soon covered in the best white sheets from a dozen households, starched and ironed to perfection and smelling like a wash day. Each family put out the plates and spoons for their children while Maggie climbed onto chairs to hang the flags and bunting across the road from tree to tree.

"It looks splendid!" commented old Mr Riley, leaning on his walking stick to survey operations as if he were still an air raid warden. Maggie thanked him as she began decorating the tables with the paper flowers the children made, and a few drops of rain splattered their way onto the paving slabs.

"I hope Elsie's remembered to collect the ice cream." Maggie's voice was beginning to sound as if she had the cares of the world on her shoulders. "It's a trek up the hill to the icehouse, if she hasn't got it down to the kitchen already."

"We're lucky the village hall has somewhere to store enough for this lot!" laughed Olive as they strung more bunting above the door.

"Just in time, Olive!" Maggie turned to see a crocodile of children marching across the grass, Lil in front, blowing her guide captain's whistle, and Joe rounding up the stragglers at the back. The adults burst into spontaneous applause at the sight of their children's happy faces, their excited whoops and cheers filling the air with the kind of noise not heard since the end of the war.

Even Lil couldn't hold her ragtag army together as they neared the tables. Some ran, skipped, or shyly walked as they descended on their allotted places with much scraping of chair legs. Out of the kitchens came what they were waiting for, and they dived on the sandwiches as if they'd starved for a week.

"Just look at them wolfing down that jelly!" laughed Olive a few minutes later as Maggie let the children's laughter wrap her in the joy of the moment.

Maggie's eyes glistened as she and Olive watched Teddy. He was still a little thin, but he sat with his brothers and sisters, grinning and clutching his balloon, throwing his head back with laughter. Maggie felt a warm sense of triumph for her friend, thinking of what might have been. Further down the table was Minnie, her legs in callipers. That disease was to be even more cruel in the epidemic that would spread throughout the middle of the decade, and Maggie would be glad she didn't have to watch a child of hers confined or crippled.

I wonder where he is now, she thought. *Is my son at a party somewhere, surrounded by love?* She instinctively touched her stomach, pushing down the old longing so that no one saw it under her common sense.

Maggie and Sam settled into a life without their own children, Maggie becoming a favourite among the young mothers of the village as she worked tirelessly to help them with their growing families. If they needed someone to look after a child for a few hours, they would call Maggie. If they needed someone to take care of the family while they went into hospital, they would call Maggie. Maggie organised get-togethers for them, baking delicious cakes and never minding holding the latest baby while a mother sorted out another child. Maggie helped at Sunday School and Brownies, and she was free to take a turn in cleaning the church or running a jumble sale. She joined the Women's Voluntary Service and helped to build a playground, and she became a pillar of the local Women's Institute.

"Ask Maggie" became a familiar answer to who was going to do whatever was needed in the community. After all, she wasn't tied down with a family.

Chapter Thirteen

1960

When Maggie accidentally fell pregnant again at thirty-four, neither she nor Sam dared to hope that this time all would be well. Maggie rested, Sam worked, and both avoided planning, naming, or talking about having a baby. They told no one for the first six months, Maggie hiding her expansion under loose cardigans and aprons. Autumn turned to winter, winter to spring, and they contained their hope and surprise as the summer approached.

Sam occasionally borrowed a shiny old black Ford car with leather seats from someone his uncle knew. The man had driven during the war and never had to pass a driving test but found the growing number of cars on the road a frightening prospect. Sam could not yet afford to buy the car, but he'd driven during his war service, so he passed his test easily. He and Maggie had found some solace in driving out to the countryside on a Sunday, down leafy lanes with overhanging trees they nicknamed "fairyland", so magical was the light that found its way through the canopy. Picnicking or walking in fields provided a soothing calm, listening to the birds instead of the voices of concern.

Finally, one beautiful day in June, Maggie knew she was about to meet the child she longed to keep safe.

"It's time, Sam!" she grinned at him, as she gripped the back of the chair.

Sam fumbled with his pullover as panic took over his whole body. He jumped on his bike and set off to get the midwife, his trembling legs held steady by the pedals and his hands resisting the urge to ring the bicycle bell all the way there. When the midwife arrived, he was banished to the living room, where he was told to make sure he kept a fire going, even if it was June.

All he could do was pace up and down the living room, then up and down the street, then all along the hall until he heard a cry. His heart leapt, and he wished he could just go up the stairs and burst through the door, but he knew the midwife would never let that happen. He would just have to wait until he was told he could go in.

The sturdy woman appeared at the top of the stairs with a huge, confident smile. "Mr Mitchell. Come and meet your daughter." She might have said more, but Sam didn't know. He took the stairs two at a time and rushed through the bedroom door, almost knocking over a jug of water. As he peered round the door, he saw his Maggie, exhausted but beaming. In her arms was a wriggling, strong, lively baby. Unsure what to do next, he leant over and kissed them both. The midwife gently lifted the infant into his arms, telling him to support it well. With trembling lips, he looked from the baby to Maggie, to the midwife and back, his eyes widening as he fought the tears of joy, hardly daring to believe that this time they might just have been lucky.

"Off you go now, Mr Mitchell. Time for baby to feed, and your wife needs to rest. Put the kettle on and make us all a cup of tea."

Dismissed, Sam floated downstairs as if in a dream and wandered out into the street. When his neighbour appeared, wiping her hands on her apron, he blurted out the news. "The baby... the baby's come, Rosie."

Her husband John appeared from the corner of the street, cricket bat in hand.

"Pop round to Nelson Street, Johnnie," Rosie called to him, "to tell them the baby's here!"

"She's beautiful, Rosie," Sam exclaimed. "She's OK, and she's beautiful!"

Rosie hugged him and told him to get back indoors. Johnnie would do as he was asked, and she would get the word round. "You go and look after your family now, Sam."

There was no question of what her name would be. *June,* of course. Born to summertime, she was to be the sunshine in their life. She was such a good baby. Maggie couldn't understand why some other mothers had babies that cried all the time. They must be getting something wrong because her June would whimper a bit when she woke and wind herself up to a pitch if she were hungry, but the rest of the time she would lie in the big pram quite contentedly, and when the pram was put out in the fresh air, she slept and slept. Sometimes, Maggie had to wake her up to feed her because, according to the clinic, she must do so every four hours.

She soon got to know more new mothers, and she threw herself into celebrating every milestone. Wheeling her happy, healthy baby round the streets to show her off was the jewel in Maggie's day, and she didn't even mind the hard work of getting the nappies clean. She found herself singing as she scrubbed them, boiled them, and proudly pegged them out on the line to dry.

As June grew, she became Maggie's companion and her father's shadow. As soon as Sam came in from work, even before he ate or drank anything, he would go to see his daughter. He sat her on his knee and told her stories and taught her songs, as reluctant for her to go to bed as she was. On Sundays, the only full day Sam had at home, the little family would walk through the woods or down the lanes as snowdrops and daffodils gave way to summer hedgerows and crops ripening. June would puff out her cheeks and blow the dandelion clocks, just as her mother had done.

The house was transformed by the noise of June and her playmates running up and down—the backdrop to whatever they did. When it came to the day June started school, Maggie held her just a little bit longer, knowing this was the beginning of separation. She looked at her tiny daughter, excited to be a big girl while dressed in her uniform that would have to wait for her to grow into it. Her neatly plaited head of hair blended into the group and disappeared into the building with the other children. Some of the mothers, often with three or four children, seemed delighted that they could now be free of at least one of them during the day, but Maggie didn't share their cheerful banter.

It was when June was nearly six years old, and Maggie assumed she would never have any more children, that she was to feel herself the luckiest woman in the world because she was pregnant again. The doctors thought she was old to be carrying another child, but she willingly submitted to them keeping a close eye on her if it meant the baby would be safe, even if she felt as if her body were not her own.

She'd worn loose smocks to disguise her shape from June because she didn't dare explain why she was getting fat. As her blood pressure rose during the last month, she was taken into hospital for bed rest. Cathy arrived two weeks early in the middle of the night, without any drama, while Sam and June were fast asleep at home. When Sam phoned the next morning, he thought he was dreaming as the midwife told him his daughter had been born at 2:45am, and mother and baby were doing well.

They brought Cathy home from the hospital and told June that she had a new sister.

June jumped up and down with glee. "Yippeeeeee! You found the baby shop!" she squealed, looking over the well-wrapped bundle. "Christine's mummy told me that's where she got Mary, but I thought you would never get me a sister to play with!"

Maggie glanced at Sam, the corner of her lip threatening to let loose a giggle. At least they felt some inward relief that they wouldn't have to come up with an explanation of their own.

June was eager to fuss over the baby, thinking she was all her own. "I'm going to help mummy with everything she needs. I'll sing to her and dance with her and talk to—oh! I'll have to teach her to talk first."

The new big sister was so excited that she skipped down the road next to the pram on the first day they took Cathy out. She was incredibly proud as she showed her off to neighbours, who all seemed to want to lean over the pram and talk in silly voices. Cathy was to be the last baby Maggie carried. Time had run out, but at least she felt her little family was complete, and she relished a second chance to prove she could be a good mother.

PART FOUR

"I wasted time, and now doth time waste me;
For now hath time made me his numbering clock:
My thoughts are minutes; and with sighs they jar
Their watches on unto mine eyes, the outward watch,
Whereto my finger, like a dial's point,
Is pointing still, in cleansing them from tears."
— **Shakespeare: Richard II**

Chapter Fourteen

Bob pulled away slowly, his mind drifting back to his encounter with Ed. The meeting had left him thinking about how his mother had been a real person, not just a name on a piece of paper. She' d lived in that house, had been someone's aunt and someone's wife, and maybe someone else's mother. He didn't see the brake lights go on at the back of the lorry in front of him until it suddenly loomed in the twilight, filling his windscreen. His feet pressed against the floor of the car so hard he could feel his calf muscles tighten. He felt time in slow motion as the bonnet inevitably slid, as if skating on ice, under the bar, and the back doors filled his vision.

A silent scream caught in his throat, his eyes widening as the horror hit him with a scraping, grinding noise until the blackness of night overcame him. When the paramedics called him back to consciousness, he tried to do as he was told, to stay with them, but his eyelids were so heavy that he drifted away, hearing voices as if they came through water. He decided he would rather just sleep...

Bob slid into a coma on the second day after his accident. Vicky sat at his bedside, praying her father would pull through. He was usually such a careful driver, but the motorcyclist who'd called the ambulance said he just seemed to slide into the back of the lorry, as if he didn't brake hard enough. The doctors could find no evidence of a heart attack or stroke, but here he was stretched out on cold, white sheets, looking like some kind of cyborg with technology taking over his body and keeping him alive. He'd been in the coma for two days now, and no one seemed to be able to tell her how long it would last, or whether he would ever recover.

Vicky clung to the fact that she'd inherited his quiet strength, and she willed him to fight for the life that was so precious to her. She had watched life slip from her mother, inch by inch, and she couldn't do that again so soon.

Her brother nervously messaged her every half hour, wondering whether to work or not, asking questions to which she had no answers. She was alternating between wringing her hands and texting him back when the police came to the hospital, adding to her dread.

"Good afternoon, Miss Thompson," one of the young constables said. "I'm very sorry to intrude at such a difficult time, but you'll understand that we have to establish exactly what happened."

"Yes, yes of course," Vicky replied, feeling panic rise in her throat, her hands shaking uncontrollably.

"From what we've been able to make out at the scene of the accident, Miss, it looks as if your father hit a patch of diesel in the road, so his car skidded when he braked. We'll get the diesel cleaned up, of course, but it seems he could only have avoided the accident if he'd seen the lorry before he hit the spill, and the lorry was waiting to turn right, so it stopped. We've taken statements from the motorcyclist and the lorry driver. You'll need to tell your insurers we've been involved. The lorry driver will be making a claim for damage, I'm afraid, so we'd advise you to let them know about your father as soon as possible. Obviously, your father's car won't be fit to drive, so it's been towed away. I know this is a lot to take in now, but here's the number to call if we can be of any assistance. There will be no further action, as it seems your father wasn't to blame for the accident, but we may need to speak to him, when he's up to it."

He handed Vicky a card her eyes couldn't focus on, and she put it in her bag. She nodded, unable to string words together, and the two constables backed away, turning swiftly, and heading for the door.

Vicky felt guilty for leaving her bewildered eight-year-old son Georgie with her neighbour. She'd desperately tried to make a sleep-over next-door sound like a treat, but the second night he protested, and she hated having to lie to her son. She couldn't bring herself to tell him her father was so seriously ill, playing it down to avoid upsetting him. Maybe she wouldn't need to upset him. Maybe her dad would come through this. All she could do was hope as the bleeps and pumping noises held him by a fragile cobweb of artificial life.

Chapter Fifteen

Huddled round the wood-burning stove, June and Cathy were reminiscing about their childhood, remembering how they used to wander up over the moor with the dogs, no one ever dreaming they were in any kind of danger. Now, June worried if one of twins was late, and she always played taxi driver rather than risk them taking the bus to town in the evening. She paid for taxis to get Libby back to university from the station.

The sisters remembered other snowy winters when they dragged out the old wooden sledge and squeezed both on it, careering down the hill towards the farmyard, startling the sheep with their whoops of pure joy. In those days, the snow didn't mean shovelling the drive to get the car out, because work was on the doorstep. Nostalgia came in huge doses, and bored by their chatter, the rest of the family had drifted off — Millie to the dining room and her own choice of television programmes, and Alex upstairs, guitar music floating through the ceiling as he struggled to master "House of the Rising Sun".

The wind was roaring down the side of the house and through the chimney, and the daffodils were bending their heads in submission. It might be nearly spring, but that news didn't seem to have reached the village yet. The smell of burning wood always brought back memories of bonfires at the bottom of the garden. Cathy's thoughts lingered on bonfire nights at the farm next door, when the children had ridden down to the middle field on bales of hay on a trailer pulled by an old tractor. How simple everything seemed then.

Cathy sensed that June's tense shoulders meant she was steeling herself for something unpleasant. Cathy was busy trying to work out how to ask her what was wrong, when suddenly, staring into the flames, June announced, "We may have to sell the house, you know."

Cathy heard the words but didn't believe she had. "What?"

"We may have to sell the house. The solicitor phoned today about the reading of Mum's will. The house may not be ours, Cathy. We may have to move."

"WHAT?"

"Stop saying *what*! It seems that someone has appeared out of nowhere since Mum died. Something about someone else being entitled to something. I don't know the details. I've been dreading telling you, and I didn't want to say anything in front of the twins."

"How on earth could that be? I don't believe it! There can't be anyone else, can there? There must be a mistake!" She felt the cosy, comfy world she'd come back to claim crumbling to ashes and dust.

"No mistake, according to Mr Smithson. He wants to see us in the morning. Nine o'clock. He has proof, he says. Oh, Cathy, what am I going to do if someone wants me to sell the house? This has been my home for so long. What about the kids? How am I going to give them the sort of house they're used to living in on what I earn? When Mark left, this was where I came back to, where we grew up, where Mum and Dad are still in the fabric of the place. I've coped, but this is just a bridge too far."

A silent tear slipped down June's cheek, shaking Cathy to the core. She wasn't used to having to be strong for June. It felt as if the world were tilting on its axis, and everything were suddenly all at the wrong angle. She reached out and touched her sister on the wrist. "We find out what we're up against, June, and we fight."

June nodded, her eyes reflecting the flickering fire as she sat rigidly immobile and expressionless, as if the flames had robbed her of her will.

Cathy fidgeted with the fringe on the cushion, eyes towards the floor, her brain spinning in its search for something to make sense of. She looked at her sister, and instinct made her ask, "There's more, isn't there?"

"Yes."

"Well come on then. What? What haven't you told me?"

"He claims he's our half-brother."

"What?"

"There you go again!"

"Sorry, but what makes him think that?"

"It seems our mother was his mother, too."

"How? When? Who? What's going on?"

June tried her best to explain. "According to Mr Smithson, Mum had a baby before she met Dad. It seems we don't know as much as we thought we knew about our parents."

The guitar music overhead stopped, and a slamming door was followed by pounding footsteps on the stairs.

"Don't say anything in front of the kids, Cathy. Nothing," June hissed urgently.

Alex came bounding through the door of the kitchen, calling out, "Anything to eat, Mum? I'm starving!"

Chapter Sixteen

Cathy fiddled with the keys in her pocket while June flicked through the pages of a magazine as they waited to be called into Mr Smithson's office. It felt like waiting to go into the dentist. Eventually, the PA clicked out of his office in her high heels, and her painted nails wrapped around a file. "Mr Smithson will see you now."

"Good morning, ladies. May I call you June and Cathy? I had so much to do with your mother while she was alive, I almost feel I know you already." His kindly smile creased his face and lit his eyes, glasses sliding to the end of his nose and his white hair standing on end as if he'd had a shock.

He wouldn't have been out of place in a Dickens novel, June thought.

"Do take a seat," he said, as they nodded their agreement. "First of all, I have a letter here to be given to you when your mother died. She instructed me to ensure that the letter is read before the will."

He handed June a brown envelope addressed to the two of them. She handed it back, as if it had scalded her palm, looking at Cathy as she did so and receiving a nod of confirmation. "Would you read it out, please, Mr Smithson?"

"Of course, if that's what you want," he replied and opened the envelope slowly and carefully, unfolding the sheet of printer paper inside. Taking a deep breath, he began:

"'My darling girls,

If you are reading this, it will be because I am no longer with you. If I have reached old age, don't grieve too long for me, my loves, because life goes by so fast in hindsight, and you must focus on living yours to the full.

I have been blessed to have had a wonderful husband in your father and two beautiful daughters who have brought me so much pride. You are very different, but each of you has such gifts and talents to offer the world that my wish for you is that you never forget, whatever life throws at you, that you are worthy of respect, loyalty, and love. Don't ever let anyone make you feel that you fall short of expectations, as you have exceeded mine.

Now, I must tell you, darlings, things that I have kept secret for very good reasons, as you have a right to know truths that may surface with my demise. Before I knew your father, I was young and foolish, and I fell in love with a handsome young fighter pilot, no older than I was. It was near the end of the war, and the world was a dangerous place, none of us knowing how long we would be allowed to survive in it. When I look back now, I wonder how those boys did what they did, but we must be eternally grateful to them. So many of them lost their lives, and that was the fate of the one I thought I would marry. One day, he flew a mission and did not return. Not long afterwards, I found myself pregnant, to the dismay of my mother and father, and I was sent away to be hidden with my aunt in Wales until I could return as if nothing had happened. My son was taken from me, and somewhere out there, my loves, is a brother you have never known. I hope that, in this day and age, you will not condemn me. How fortunate, today, are girls in love, with access to the pill and the ability to keep their babies even if they are not married. I don't think my father ever forgave me my shame. Your father is the only other person who knew about my past, and he understood. I had several miscarriages before we were lucky enough to have you two, as well. Perhaps, Cathy, knowing this, you will understand more readily, how painful it was to lose you, too, when you went abroad.

I have never had the opportunity to find my son or to tell him that I loved him but had no choice. Now, I am going to my maker acknowledging that I have three children, which of course He knows already. I don't know whether my baby will ever be found, but in case he is, or in case he finds you, I need him to know that he was never forgotten. He was always in my heart, along with you. I am, therefore, leaving him a legacy in my will.

June, you have been my rock since your father died, and your children have brought back the sunshine you brought into our lives with your arrival. I thank you for that, from the bottom of my heart. You need to be secure in the place they know, and I know that our home is your home. You are to be able to live in the house for the rest of your life if you want to, no matter who owns what part of it, without paying anything other than maintenance costs, as if it were just your own.

Cathy, your life is not here. You have made a new life, and sometimes there has not been much room for us in it. I know you love us, but your reality is one that takes you across the world where you have other loves, too. You have done such wonderful things in your career, and you have been so very successful. You have earned more than your father and I could have dreamt of earning. But you have paid a price, haven't you? I can't put right for you what has gone wrong, but you do not need me to provide financial stability, so instead I am leaving you my photograph albums, so that you have with you a little of your old home and your past when you are back in Australia. Your past is the foundation on which you have been able to build your present. Now, you must decide what kind of future you want, so that you can find the contentment you don't seem to have reached so far.

You will have guessed, I am sure, that I am duty-bound to split what I have between you all. This will be formally set out in the will, but I am explaining here.

The smallholding was the product of your father's hard work, and although I inherit what is his, I acknowledge that it is more his than mine and therefore more his children's than anyone else's.

June is to be custodian of the house and smallholding for as long as she is able and willing. This is on the assumption that Cathy will continue to want to visit it from time to time, so she will have the use of it for the duration of June's custody. When June relinquishes it, alive or dead, and it is sold, the proceeds are to be divided unequally, to take account of the investment of time, upkeep, and care put in by June. June is to have half, the whole of your father's half. The other half is to be divided between three of you on condition that those due to inherit are prepared to contribute to the upkeep of the property, bearing a share of any major works needed. If my son cannot be traced, this will revert to three-quarters and a quarter ownership by the two of you.

Should any heirs not be prepared to accept the conditions, they are to be released from their obligation on condition that they relinquish their inheritance.

I hope you will understand my wishes. My own personal possessions you must sort out between yourselves, just the two of you, but I know there will be something Cathy will find as a keepsake, something easy to transport.

I must say a final "goodbye," my darlings, and that is hard to do, as I know it will be for you. My final wish is that you stay in touch, however far apart you may be, because to have each other is so important. You share memories that bind you together, and you must make more. Cathy, get that sister of yours out to visit you, especially if, as I suspect, Libby takes off in your wake. Be kind to each other. Love each other, as I have loved you. God bless. Xxxx'"

Stunned, Cathy and June looked at each other, saying nothing. The pause seemed to last for minutes, broken only by Mr Smithson's gentle prompting. "You understand that a letter is only a statement of wishes, and what is legally binding is the will, to which we must now turn. I'm sure your mother wanted you to be able to understand why she'd made the bequeaths she made, but it must be something of a shock to you both if you had no idea what happened in the past."

"No, no we didn't know," stumbled June. "We knew nothing until your phone call, Mr Smithson. It will all take a bit of sinking in, I think."

"Of course. Let's now hear what the will itself says, shall we? Or do you need to go away and come back another time for that?"

"No. We'll hear it now, please," interjected Cathy. "We need to know everything, so that we know what we're dealing with." She looked at June who nodded in agreement.

Mr Smithson opened the envelope on his desk, carefully and slowly, adjusting his glasses and preparing for a very formal delivery of what he knew was going to be difficult to hear.

Cathy and June heard every word but took in little of the detail, other than what they had already learnt from the letter. Maggie had left each of the children something, the twins' inheritance to be held in a trust fund until their eighteenth birthdays. She had also left money in one of her ISAs to her favourite charity. Her jewellery was to be left to June, with the exception of one ring to be chosen by Cathy. All her other possessions, including the car and the contents of the house were to be left to Cathy and June to sort out between themselves, keeping what they wanted to keep and disposing of anything else as they saw fit. Beyond this, any monies she had in savings or investments were to be equally split between Cathy and June. The property was indeed willed to all of them, including her son, should he ever be found, so that he would always know he was not forgotten.

"Rest assured I will take care of all the legal formalities, and your mother's estate will have my personal attention. As soon as title deeds and other documents are in order, I'll be in touch. I do hope you'll be able to move forward with sorting out the rest of her possessions. I know it's a difficult task for anyone, but don't worry—you can leave me to deal with anything that's not straightforward."

Wishing them "good luck," he stood to shake their hands. "Your mother was a truly lovely lady," he smiled.

"So now we know. Some stranger gets to muscle in on what our mother left." The bitterness was thinly veiled in Cathy's comment. "That's your home, June! How could she?"

"I can't quite believe it, Cathy! Why didn't we know? How could she have kept that from us till now? We have a brother somewhere!"

Chapter Seventeen

As Cathy began to settle into the routine of comings and goings, walking the dogs and sharing memories, she eked out her savings by doing shifts behind the bar at the local pub, finding comfort in the sense of belonging and the superficial geniality that shielded her from questioning herself. She kept in contact with Jim and her secretary, leaving them to run the business without her and hoping that she would eventually feel able to go back or sell it.

January slipped away. Maybe she would just stay in this safe cocoon. She avoided deciding anything, allowing herself to just be a part of her sister's household, suffocating the knowledge that she must, at some stage, get beyond this numbing pretence and sort out permanence of some kind. In her mind, she had come home, but seeping through the dam she had mentally built between illusion and reality was the realisation that the past, though ever present in the memory of her formative years, was not the present. She'd come back to the same village expecting it to wrap itself around her like a comfort blanket, but it was not the same village, and its evolution was bound to disappoint her. It tarnished her memory to see the comings and goings at the Hall, the shifting social hierarchy that had been a kind of stability.

"How do you cope with all this change?" Cathy asked her sister. "All the builders seem to want to build are large, detached commuter-occupied houses. What chance do the young have of affording to live here now?"

"Not a hope," was June's reply. "It's just as bad for the elderly, with the bus services disappearing and families moving away. As the farms disappear, it's not the same community. But it's home. I still love the place. I belong here!" June shrugged her shoulders with a resignation Cathy couldn't equal.

"It just seems out of balance somehow, doesn't it?" Cathy sensed that pressing the point would make her sound like the outsider she now was, and she beat a tactful retreat to her room. She began to feel the discomfort of trying to recapture something that had been turned out and driven away. She was drawing on memories, drifting between past and present, but not embedding them in a future.

If I'm going to get back to reality, Cathy realised, *I've got to accept the way things are. I'm not the same person.* She began to realise that to find herself amidst the whirlwind of her thoughts, she had to reconcile the memories with what she'd become. She would have to see herself as others saw her and find a way to merge that girl who ran across the fields with the wind in her hair with the woman whose pursuit of perfection controlled her life and fearfully eliminated spontaneity. What this place had given her back was a freedom from her diary and routine, and she realised she had no idea what the weekend would bring. She was learning, again, to let life happen.

When Cathy appeared in a pair of stone-washed jeans and a baggy fleece borrowed from June's plentiful supply—hair scraped back in a clip and her feet in a pair of trainers—Millie's startled eyes almost betrayed her amazement. "You look different, Auntie Cathy," she commented, focusing carefully on her toast. "Are you doing something special?"

"Now that the roads are better, and it's such a beautiful crisp day, I'm going to borrow your grandmother's old Land Rover and get myself out into the Dales. I'm going for a walk. I might be out some time. Would you tell your mum when she gets back from shopping?"

"OK. Enjoy!" Munching the last mouthful of toast, Millie ran up the stairs, feeling in danger of choking. She burst into Alex's room, where he was playing air drums to whatever was coming through his headphones. Responding to his sister's frantic gesticulation, he removed the headphones, to ask what the emergency was.

"OMG, Alex! You should see Auntie Cathy! I think she's cracking up! She's in JEANS and a scruffy sweater, and she hasn't done her hair, and she's going WALKING!"

The dogs set up a hopeful whining, as they sensed someone was going out, but their excitement was short-lived. Cathy ignored their pacing up and down and strode purposefully straight past them. She clambered into the driving seat of the battered old green Land Rover, crunching sounds making her cringe as she reminded herself how to drive without an automatic gearbox. *As long as I don't have to reverse, I think I'll be OK,* she told herself. *Thank heavens for automatics! I haven't driven anything like this for years!*

"Come on, old thing," she encouraged it, shooting forward like a learner on her first driving lesson, letting the clutch out too fast and launching herself into the road with more determination than skill. She narrowly missed a cyclist on the bend, and the farmer driving his cattle in the opposite direction threw expletives at her as she jerked forward and almost steered into his five-bar gate. She didn't dare stop in case she couldn't pull away on the hill. She waved at him and smiled, hoping he wouldn't bear a grudge.

"Bloody women drivers!" she read on his lips as he waved his arm at her and steered a cow out of her path.

It felt good driving down the deserted lanes, the car windows open and the cold, fresh air wafting across her face. The sun was doing its best to look as if it were already spring in a steel-blue, cloudless sky. Cathy hadn't been here since before she emigrated, but there was something settling about the permanence of the stone of walls and cottages and the pattern of the fields, just as they had been then. She hadn't allowed herself, young as she'd been, to miss this landscape, but now she felt the old connection creeping its way into her soul, lifting it with its comforting message that it was still here, a safety net in her world of change. Past, present, and future met in these hills and valleys, and they took her back as if she were still nineteen and free.

She parked the car and studied the map on the board nearby.

O.K. What have we got here? Three paths from the car park—one seems to go through woods, one across fields, and one a nature trail along the river. Well, I haven't walked far for a very long time, but so what? I feel like being on top of a hill today, and I don't want to meet anyone, so let's try the longest route. I just hope the woods aren't too creepy. Cathy approached the bridge across the river, realising as she stepped on it that it bounced a little. This would, ordinarily, scare her into going back, but the only access to the footpath was across the bridge, and today she was determined to get to the other side.

She stopped halfway, looking up and down the river that flowed fast after all the melting snow and rain. The sheer beauty of the white rocks proudly standing on the banks — water lapping over those it hid — and the majesty of the trees flanking the torrent flooded her senses with a kind of calm she hadn't known for so long. She felt guilty for enjoying it when her mother had only just been laid to rest, yet she felt relief that here she could leave behind everything else and just immerse herself in being a part of this world of living things.

Cathy looked up through the trees on her right, where the sun split into knife-sharp rays piercing through the bare branches, inviting her to tackle the steep steps ahead of her. The warning on the map-board said that there were 232 of them on the route, but she didn't care. She set off with determination, carefully avoiding the tree roots that claimed their ancient right to criss-cross the makeshift footpath and log-edged steps.

As she reached the top of the ridge, she took a deep breath and looked across the valley. Remnants of snow still sat on the tops of the distant hills, but below that, spread out before her, was the patchwork of fields and walls that had endured years and years of turning seasons. She envied the certainty of that annual round, even in the face of what could be yearly disaster at the mercy of the weather. Whatever was happening around the world, whatever the stock market did, or the money-makers worried about, there they were, these beautiful fields full of promise. Deserted as they were, she wondered at the fact that most people just never saw them while they were crammed into their housing estates and jetting off to somewhere warm for a holiday. It wasn't that she didn't love where she lived in Australia, but she realised she never really appreciated England's "green and pleasant land" when she was young.

Cathy walked along the ridge noticing the trees, their gnarled bark testament to their age, and she began to see faces in the patterns, just as she had as a child. She wrapped her arms around one huge tree to check its size and smiled as she remembered how she and June would each find a tree to measure and see which was the biggest, fattest oak. Now, it almost felt as if the trees were wrapping their arms around her.

As she rounded a bend, she began the descent back towards the river, and she could hear the rush of water. Sunlight struck the surface like fairy gold reflected in shards of light that dazzled her eyes. The water tumbled over the rocky weir with foam-tipped energy. Captivated, she sat on a tree stump and let her mind wander.

A thought began to creep into Cathy's consciousness and refused to go away. Confronted with the knowledge that her mother had been forced to give up her son, she began to unravel what it must have been like to be her—not just her mother specifically, but someone who had a past, a life, scars of loss and emotions she knew nothing about. She still remembered the day she broke the news to her mother that she was leaving the country. She'd dreaded doing it, knowing her mother would be devastated, but it had to be done.

Cathy waited until her parents were comfortable in front of the television, steeled herself, and blurted, "Mum, Dad, I'm going to Australia. I've been offered a job, and I'm going to take it. I'm just sorting everything out, and when my visa comes through, I'll be off, probably just after Christmas." She avoided making eye contact, but in her peripheral vision she saw her mother's frame seem to shrink into the armchair—arms clutched around her stomach as if holding herself.

Silence seemed to last an age until her father said with a steady voice, "Well, if you've got a terrific opportunity, I don't blame you. Nothing to stay here for, is there?" He sat on the edge of his chair, deceiving himself as well as her.

Cathy hadn't disagreed. She could feel the shock radiating from her mother's taut body and breaking voice. Now she couldn't remember what her mother said, or the attempts to ask some feeble questions. All she saw in her mind's eye was the silent tears running slowly down her mother's face, and the feeling that everything had been transformed into slow motion. She recalled how they hugged, and her mother's instruction: "Go, before I cry."

Later, June had told Cathy what their father had seen. As she went out, her mother collapsed against the kitchen units, sobbing like someone whose dearest loved one had just died, incapable of anything but cries of "No! Oh God, NO!" Maggie had known that if her daughter made up her mind, that would be it. She would go. Engulfed by imminent loss and ultimate fear of what the future held, Maggie clung to her husband, who—helpless in the face of such grief—could say nothing to make it any better. Their world as they expected it to be was falling apart, and Sam couldn't hold it together for her now. Her baby, and any future grandbabies, would be across the unfathomable oceans of the world, along with the piece of her ripped from her very being at this moment in time.

Years later, Cathy said to a friend, "When I was young, I just wanted a different life. I didn't realise what I'd done to my parents, especially Mum." Caring about it had only gone so far. It was only now, with her mother no longer just always there if she chose to visit, that she felt so keenly the time they had not had, the love she missed. In so many years, she had probably only actually spent a total of weeks with the one person who had loved her unconditionally, even when her heart was breaking. She had chosen to believe in her father's bravado because it was easier than realising it was false. She had never acknowledged her mother's grief, and she certainly hadn't allowed her to talk about it. She'd never even allowed herself to miss her old life too much, throwing herself into her new one and enjoying all that it had to offer. A tinge of sadness had surfaced from time to time, especially when others spoke of visiting family, but that was what she missed, with no acknowledgment of her parents' feelings. She'd taken her choice and made the best of it, making her pilgrimage to see them when she could. She'd spent a few days with them every couple of years when she visited England and done the rounds. Life had taken on its own routines, and she'd made new friends who filled her life with their social calendar while work consumed her days, weeks, months, and years until her norm had no place for missing them or feeling guilt.

Now, knowing grief, she wished she could have understood more, cared more, made more time to pick up the phone—wanted her mother as much as her mother wanted her, instead of pushing her to the back of her mind while she got on with her job and her life. Too late now to prize that love she had taken for granted. Too late to ask how her mother felt or to give her any comfort. Push people away and time slips through your fingers, and they're gone.

Cathy began to think about what it must have felt like to have that hole in your life for so long. She began to think about the love a mother has for her child, a love that can be unselfish, however painful that may be. She began to think about the need a child has for a mother, even when that child is old enough to be a mother, an aunt, a grandfather. She began to see that her mother had held the love for her son in her heart all those years and had needed to tell him that in her will. He was still her son.

As she climbed back into the car, it was as if the river had been in an enchanted wood where she'd seen glimpses of the past, glimpses of the separate person her mother had been. It was almost as if she could see her in her head, reaching out through the sunlight, across the chasm in her understanding.

Chapter Eighteen

Vicky watched George drawing a picture of the queen in his school project book. He'd become fascinated by the idea of a family tree, and he wished he were descended from a king. She'd never really thought about heredity or ancestry, but she noticed how her dad hesitated when Georgie asked him for a photo of his great grandma. She'd found one of Peggy for him, and he stuck it into his scrapbook and carefully labelled it. Then she found one of her granddad, looking up and smiling as he was caught making something in his shed. She remembered this gentle, kind man, always making something and delighting in presenting it to his grandchildren. Robert had often sat her on his knee when she was George's age and quietly retold old stories or recited nursery rhymes.

"Two little dickie-birds, sitting on a wall. One named Peter. One named Paul. Fly away Peter. Fly away Paul..."

How different it was now with Georgie looking things up on the internet and playing electronic games—that innocent, slow exchange of old rhymes and old games disappearing in the face of immediate answers and quick responses. Vicky welcomed the genealogy project, a warm feeling of rightness creeping over her when she took Georgie to see Bob. Georgie proudly showed him the queen's family tree, asking again about his own. He had got her thinking, too, about who came before Peggy and Robert.

She began to wonder about family traits, as she had, somehow, always been destined to be a teacher—the desire in her from early youth. She had also loved to travel to places that made her mother lose sleep at night, and she relished the excitement of learning to fly at the local gliding club.

Vicky's brother had always been artistic but organised and running his own company had made him self-sufficient at an early age. People often expected them to be the same since they were close as children, but they were definitely not two peas in a pod. Unlike anyone else in the family, Mike had striking, thick, raven-black hair that he wore like a prize, styled to enhance his strong profile and to lure the girls into his trap. There was something of an Italian Romeo in his looks, and he knew when he was making himself irresistible. His friends egged him on, laughing as he made another conquest or left some poor female devastated.

Vicky's blue eyes were like her father's, her hair fair to sandy. Had she cared about make-up and fashion, she would have been equally as striking as her brother, but she refused to be driven into the conventional mould of the glossy magazines. She was happier in her jeans and trainers than some of the ridiculous clothes and shoes the fashion gurus would have women wear, and while she would don a trouser suit for work, she was not going to wear skirts when she didn't have to.

Her mother had encouraged her to be fiercely independent, which was probably why she'd never contacted Georgie's father to tell him a baby was on its way. She was never sure whether she made the right decision, but then she was never sure that she knew anything about the man she slept with one night on holiday. She'd regretted it the following morning and was perfectly happy, at the time, not to see him again, but she felt dreadful the next day and suspected that her drink had been spiked, although she had no proof. The wedding party on the beach, under the stars, had been fuelled with flowing wine, glasses filled before she even realised they were half-empty.

The man certainly hadn't made any attempt to find her, and she knew she'd just been a one-night stand—enjoyed and forgotten. When she became pregnant, she realised that maybe an abortion would have been the sensible option, but Mum had understood her decision completely, and she'd been there during the sleepless nights of Georgie's first few months, taking turns so that Vicky could get some rest. Her parents had been the best, and she missed her mum every time she wished she could talk to her about Georgie's latest wonderful skill.

It crossed her mind that if Georgie was going to have a proper family tree, he should be looking at her mother's ancestors too, but for now, she thought she should have asked her dad to record some of his memories while he still could. When he was better, she must ask him, before it was too late. It was only occasionally that he talked about his parents and his youth, and suddenly she realised that we expect our parents always to have been our parents and not to have been young. Vicky'd taught enough literature to have had to think about the society in which the characters lived, but somehow this never connected with knowing about where her own ancestors fitted into those worlds. Maybe she could do some digging while he was in hospital and present it to her dad for his next birthday. Both of her parents had been only children, so there couldn't be that much to discover. She knew her father had been looking on web sites for information, so if she just went into his history on his PC, she'd know which ones they were.

With Bob in safe hands, Vicky gave herself permission to take a break from her vigil by his bedside. His stone-built semi looked forlorn as she pulled up outside, but his neighbour had obviously been kind enough to cut the grass in the front garden, so at least it didn't lower the tone of the respectable neighbourhood. She let herself in, went into the study, and booted up the computer. *Oh, it was so slow! Why did he still use this old thing?* she wondered. It came to life, the virus checker telling her it was doing a scan, and at last she was able to click on history. She typed the names of the websites into the notes page on her phone, ready for later, then shut down the PC. As she was leaving the room, an uneven pile of paper on the windowsill caught her eye. It wasn't like her father to leave anything untidy; it would drive him mad.

She reached out to straighten the pile, noticing letters and numbers on the top page, and said to herself, "What's this, then?" It seemed to be some marriage dates for people called Harrison and Mitchell. Intrigued, she moved the top piece of paper, and an envelope fell to the floor.

Vicky knew she should just put it back, but curiosity got the better of her. She carefully opened the envelope, almost feeling as if she should look away as she did so, and slid the contents out onto the desk. The marriage certificate Bob had received just before his accident stared at her, daring her to take a closer look. She knew she was going to abandon her high moral principles, and she was ceasing to care! She opened the document fully, and the same names as those on the printout jumped out at her. Margaret Catherine Harrison. Samuel Alexander Mitchell. So, who were they?

She went back to the pile of papers, glancing at what her father had obviously found through his own research. As she shifted pages, she saw another envelope—this one yellow with age.

Ten minutes later, Vicky took a few deep breaths, the rush of blood to her cheeks and her shaking hands signalling the realisation that her son had not been the only one trying to trace the past. She knew, now, that her father had made a momentous discovery that must have rocked him to the core. She couldn't remember how she found out that he and her mother had both been adopted, but somehow, she knew. She'd always thought that was something they had in common, that it had strengthened their relationship.

Bob had told her, years ago, that his birth mother had died having him, and that was why he was so protective of her when she was pregnant. No one had gone into lengthy explanations, but her mother had been adamant that Georgie was to grow up in his own family, if that's what Vicky had wanted.

Yet Bob had told her nothing of these latest discoveries. *Was he going to tell me?* she wondered. *Was he waiting until he was certain? Was he hurting too much to talk about it?* He didn't talk about his feelings, and she knew he would need to come to terms with his discoveries before he would discuss them in his matter of fact-I'm-quite-all-right way.

You could think you had left the past behind you, but here it was alive, dancing its devil tune in the present, opening scars as if it prepared to drink their blood.

For his sake, she knew she could say nothing while he was still frail. It was better that this was buried for a little longer. She put the pile back exactly as she'd found it and closed the door quietly on her way out, as if she were afraid her father would hear her.

As the days trickled by, the bruises on Bob's cheeks faded from deep purple to yellowish green, and his eyes fluttered like butterfly wings as he heard a familiar voice. Vicky was delighted when it seemed her father was responding to external stimuli—a groan following the prick of a needle or a slight twitch as she touched his hand.

After two anxious weeks, Mike flew in to find his father propped up and awake, eyelids heavy and gaze unfocused. He wasn't sure that Bob knew he was there, but at least he satisfied himself that he was not about to be dealing with his death. He loved his father dearly, but he had a company to run, and there were things that would not wait. After making his perfunctory appearance, he hugged his sister and his nephew—promising to return at the end of the month—and took his leave, heading back to his London office.

Vicky was left in no doubt that she would be the one to juggle work and her father's needs, taken for granted because she'd always been there. She had been able to spend the half-term holiday visiting every day, sometimes bringing Georgie with her and sometimes accepting invitations for him to go to play with his friends. She didn't want him to have to see his granddad like this. She needed to protect him as long as she could. The hospital was no place for him; he was a boy full of energy, needing to be occupied, and the visiting rules meant he couldn't always be allowed on the ward. She was delighted when Bob was eventually out of bed and out of danger, and she could allow Georgie the excitement of Granddad coming home.

Bob was a fighter. He'd lived his motto of "never give up", and the joy in his grandson's eyes was enough to spur him on. As a teenager, his parents had taken him to a naval open day, never anticipating how that would determine so much of his future. Lured by the promise of adventure and skills for life, he was fired with enthusiasm and determination to sign up for a life in the Royal Navy.

He gained a place at Dartmouth and set his heart on sailing the seas. Nothing was going to hold back the boy whose resolve was absolute. The navy had been the first love of his life, and even when he finally retired, it seemed the navy never left him. His clothes were always neat and conventional, his shoes shining until they reflected whatever was around them. He ironed his own shirts and pressed his own trousers so they would be just so, despite protestations that he didn't have to do that when he was home. Somehow, even when he wore an old jumper and his slippers, he never lost the bearing that marked him as the officer he had become. His life was busy and purposeful, even after the tragedy of widowerhood, whether that was working for the charity he'd adopted or travelling up and down the country to various associations connected with his naval days. He had given Vicky a list of people to notify that he was out of action, and the cards came flooding in as the word spread.

As Bob gained in strength, old comrades appeared to visit him, and they entertained the rest of the ward with their tales of places they'd been and experiences they had lived. Even as a pensioner, it was clear that he could charm his way into anyone's good books, and Vicky could see why her mother had fallen in love with him all those years ago and been prepared to put up with his absences. It was only becoming a mother herself that had given her the insight into their relationship that had been beyond her when she was a child. Growing up, they'd just been Mum and Dad, but in adulthood she was able to see beyond that to the life they had before she and Mike existed. It was weird, thinking of not existing, but her mother had been someone who squirreled away mementos, and every now and then she would sit down with Vicky and tell her about the stories attached to them. It had seemed that the past was full of important dates and times and places, and Vicky had loved the stories behind the ornaments or pictures or photographs, all of them somehow involving her father.

Vicky's mother had always seemed to be at peace with what had been, so that she had an obvious contentment with the present—until she was ill. She loved life and loved them, and she fought as hard as she could, for as long as she could. Even in her last days in the hospice, she had held Vicky's hand and told her not to have any regrets, but to see what passed as adding to the experience that was life. Vicky tried to emulate that positivity and strength, knowing that Bob's devotion was going to devastate him. Caroline had been his best friend, as well as his wife, and facing a future of old age without her was not what he'd anticipated.

Chapter Nineteen

Vicky struggled to secure the enormous Christmas tree on the roof rack of her car, pine needles poking her wrists where her coat sleeves had pulled away from the edge of her gloves. She was determined that this was going to be the best Christmas ever, and they were going to celebrate getting her father out of hospital.

Bob's house had stood empty for weeks, and the chill grabbed her as she set foot through the front door. Georgie ran past, opening doors and bringing life back into the gloom.

"Bring it in, Mum! Hurry up! Let's put it in this corner here!"

"OK, Georgie. Hang on a minute! I've got to untie it first! Can you get me the scissors from the kitchen drawer?" Vicky didn't really need the scissors because she had tied the string in bows, but she did need to catch her breath and steady herself, fixing the smile on her face for when Georgie returned. The Bob who was coming out of hospital was not the Bob who got in the car that day. He put on a brave face, but she knew he would tire easily, and he would be walking with a frame, at least for a while, unsteady as he was.

She was bringing him back to his own house, but only because a package of care meant that someone would be coming in to help him, and she knew she was going to have to find the time and the energy to ensure that he was all right without fussing. If he suspected too much fretting or fawning over him, he would refuse help. In the discussion over his discharge, he'd already said, "I'm old enough not to need people poking their noses into my daily life. I'll be fine, *just fine*, once I get out of this place."

Vicky was grateful he was well enough to be stubborn, but that didn't alleviate the fear that clutched her insides.

Georgie returned with the scissors, and she sent him into the house with the stand for the tree. Then, together they moved the armchair from the corner of the room and put the tree in its place.

"Wow! I bet it's bigger than Tom's tree, Mum! It's touching the ceiling!" The grin on Georgie's face made Vicky genuinely smile for the first time in weeks.

"Come on, then. Let's get the decorations in and make it look fantastic!" suggested Vicky. "But first, let's get some heat going, shall we?"

An hour later, not only did the tree look "awesome," but they were peeling off layers of clothing because the heating and effort had made them both feel as if they'd run a few miles. To Vicky's relief, the tree lights worked as soon as they were switched on, for a change. Once the branches had been set free from the netting, they were able to see they needed two sets to deck this tree—much to Georgie's delight. When they'd put as many baubles and crackers and chocolates as they could on the tinsel-wrapped tree, they started on the ceiling. Georgie's insistence on paper chains soon had the whole room looking like Santa's grotto. They even wrapped tinsel round the drooping cheese plant and Georgie's hand-made Welcome Home sign was the last thing to be added. He carefully stuck it across the banisters to be seen as soon as Bob came through the door.

When they were finally sure they could do no more to make it look festive, they made their way home, warmed by their feeling of satisfaction, despite the descending frost. Their efforts were rewarded with a full moon lighting the dark sky, and the stars seemed to twinkle their approval. Vicky knew her father would both love and hate it. He'd love that it broadcast Christmas, loud and clear, and hate that it was as tacky and as fussy as they could possibly make it—totally unlike his usual token of some fairy lights and a tiny tree.

At last, Bob came home. That Christmas, they clung to each other, Mike coming to stay. All of them determinedly pulled crackers to read the tasteless jokes, sang along with the Christmas Album, which they knew so well, and filled themselves with food and memories to keep. Vicky invited friends and neighbours in for drinks and snacks and playmates for Georgie, and they were able to go out for a ride in the crisp, dry air, even if they couldn't go for a walk.

By New Year, as Mike departed, there was hope of a better year to come. Bob's new laptop was set up with Skype, so that Vicky could see him, if she couldn't get to him, and so that he could call Mike now and then. His old friends were already organising lifts to social events, until he could drive again, and Bob was suggesting a nostalgic trip to Cornwall—something for them all to look forward to.

Vicky felt a huge sense of relief to hear him being so positive, and she began planning their trip before he could change his mind. She wasn't sure where this sudden idea of revisiting her mother's county had come from, but she'd always loved their visits to Cornwall when her grandparents had been alive, and she knew the sea air would do them all good, even if it were to be in spring, rather than the height of summer.

She wished Georgie could have had the freedom she had down there. Though the detailed memory of the house and garden had faded with time, the feeling of space had not. The rambling old house had seemed enormous to her, and the garden was always full of summer, with a riot of cottage garden flowers—like Hollyhocks as tall as she was—and trees just right for climbing or hanging a rope swing. She smiled as she thought about how she and Mike would make a den near the old shed, serving each other meals of grass on paper plates and imaginary cups of tea—sheets strung over ropes, providing them with cover. She'd been lucky with grandparents, she realised, though she went through the sadness of losing them and the trauma of coming face-to-face with mortality at a young age. Georgie had no contact with one set of his, and with her mother gone, there was only her father to show him that special warmth and indulgence that had wrapped itself around her with love and pride.

Chapter Twenty

"Well, are you ready, then?" June asked, knowing full well that neither of them relished the task ahead. She sensed that Cathy was struggling with her thoughts and emotions, and she'd gone noticeably quiet over the last few days. They hadn't really discussed the visit to the solicitor because June had been plunged into the beginning of term, and she was marking mock exam papers every evening—shut away in the room she'd turned into a kind of study upstairs.

When Cathy wasn't working at the pub in the evenings, she spent them curled up watching the television while the rest of the household got on with their lives as normally as possible. It wasn't normal, of course, and they all knew it but said nothing. There was no Maggie appearing with her hot chocolate at exactly nine-thirty in the evening and announcing that she was going to bed as soon as the news started at ten. There was no Maggie waiting for them when they arrived home from school or work, wondering how their day had been and asking them what she may have asked them yesterday, or the day before. They hadn't realised how much of their time had included her, until now.

June had been sliding into being her mother's carer, making sure she took her pills when she should, sorting her clothes, writing down precise instructions for what she could do about dinner. The shift had been imperceptibly slow, and neighbours were organised to do spot checks when Maggie was left on her own. It had become routine for June to sit down with her when she got in from work, Maggie making her a cup of coffee and eagerly listening to an account of the day.

June found she could not, would not, sit down for coffee now. If Cathy were around, she would often have started dinner, and June would grab a drink and take over or take it upstairs, sipping it while she changed or checked what she had to do that evening. Cathy noticed June was going through the motions of going to work and coming home, but neither of them dared to give a voice to the feelings of loss that permeated even the simplest tasks, like clearing away the cups.

"Let's get it over and done with," answered Cathy, "while the twins are out. Ye Gods, when was the last time either of us went up into the loft, June? We must have been children! Let's hope the ladder's still in one piece!"

Neither of them knew for sure what was in the loft, but they knew years ago their father had put down boarding to make a floor because there were things to be stored up there indefinitely. They'd glimpsed a box of trophies from the days when their father had entered his vegetables into competitions, and they'd heard their mother talk about her memory chest, where she would store birthday cards once she had reread every one at least three times. They had once been up there, but they were incredibly young, and everything had seemed enormous from the beams to the old tea chests their parents had used when they moved into the house.

June carried a stool up to the landing, and Cathy climbed it to release the hatch to the opening. She stepped down, coughing as dust descended on her from inside the loft. After some manoeuvring, she grabbed the end of the ladder and pulled it down towards the floor.

June watched anxiously as Cathy clambered up the rungs into the darkness above them. "There's a light switch somewhere, isn't there?" June called up. "I think it was round to the right."

"Bingo!" called Cathy as the flickering fluorescent tube came to life and its glow steadied. "Wow, June! I'd forgotten how vast this place is! Dad must have boarded it all out over the years. Come on up!"

"I can't stand climbing ladders. Are you sure there's somewhere to put my feet? Will I be able to get myself back down?"

"It's fine, just like a floor, June. You've got to get up and see what's up here! It's like an Aladdin's cave!"

Tentatively, June put her first foot on the bottom of the ladder. As she paused, she looked down at the landing, then with a determination that outshone her courage, she grabbed the sides of the ladder and plunged towards the hatch as if dashing to catch a bus in the rain. As her head emerged in the harsh light, she dared to look upwards. It was certainly like a cave, shadows in corners and huge cobwebs hanging between rafters, as if the spiders were telling her she was entering their domain.

A long space, punctuated by the solid, old beams, was half-full of a mixture of tea chests and cardboard boxes—many looking as if they'd been there since before June was born. At the far end she could see an old bookcase and on it what looked like a well-ordered collection of leather-bound books. Next to it was a small chest of drawers decorated with transfers of Disney characters. Somewhere in her memory she saw it sitting in the corner of the nursery she, then Cathy, had occupied.

So that was where it went! June thought.

Along one of the long walls, right under the eaves, she could make out a huge trunk that had been used when they were on holiday as children. It had been so exciting when it arrived at their destination and she and Cathy could witness the opening of the trunk and find out what Mum had packed inside. There was always something new to play with, and there were always some new clothes, and hidden somewhere in the bottom would be a treat for them if they had been good on the journey. She gingerly placed one foot, then the other, onto the boarding as Cathy scrabbled in the shadows to her right, producing a handbag they both remembered from Sundays in church.

"It's like the story of our lives up here, isn't it?" ventured Cathy. "I had no idea they kept so much."

"Nor me," answered June. "Where do we start? I suppose we should see what some of these boxes have got in them."

"It looks as if the boxes have been labelled, June. Look at this one. 'Old lampshades,' as if they might just come in handy one day."

"Yes, and this one says, 'Tax Accounts,' so it looks as if one side of the room is papers, the other redundant items they didn't throw away. What about that chest over there? Do you remember that going to Norfolk with us?"

"Oh, my goodness, yes! Let's go and have a look at the books and the chest."

June regained her composure as she felt the solid boarding under her feet, and ducking under the rafters, she made her way to the far end of the attic, her eyes scanning what she passed. She could make out an old heater, a roll of carpet, a box labelled "toys" and a violin case. She had forgotten that her father had said he once played the fiddle, as he called it, in a life before she was born. *Why hadn't he played it since?* June thought, but it was only fleeting, and she quickly moved on.

As Cathy passed her, she focused on their goal, and they descended on the chest together, like two excited schoolgirls looking for their treats. They each unlatched a lock, delighted, and relieved that they needed no key to open their treasures.

June and Cathy looked into each other's eyes for a few seconds, each of them seeing the reflection of their own anticipation and apprehension, then simultaneously lifted the heavy lid, expecting it to creak as if it were in some gothic story. It didn't. It opened as easily as if it had been opened yesterday, flying upwards quickly and scattering dust behind it.

Across the top of the contents was a layer of tissue paper, carefully placed. It made a shushing sound as they moved it, making them feel like intruders. Whatever was in there, it must have been something their mother wanted to protect. They sat back on their heels, each of them reluctant to be the first one to reach in, feeling as if they were plundering an Egyptian tomb. Cathy slowly peeled back a folded cloth. She could see, even in the limited light at this end of the room, that it was beautifully embroidered. She'd never seen it before, so it had obviously been too special to be used every day. She put some of the tissue paper on the chest of drawers and carefully lay the cloth on top. As she did so, a piece of paper fell out of the folds, June catching it as it fluttered through the air. Distinctive handwriting in faded ink— a shade of sepia like an old photograph—revealed the source of the cloth.

"To my dear niece, on her engagement."

All these years, Maggie had kept it for a special occasion, but it had been too special to use at all, and she would never have the chance to use it now. Cathy remembered the post that went round Facebook every now and then, telling everyone to wear their best clothes, use their best things... June put the note with the cloth, and they turned their attention to the shoeboxes piled in the chest. June took one, Cathy another, and they gave each other unspoken permission to lift the lids.

June's box was full of cards—birthday and Christmas varieties, all from Maggie's brother. She must have kept every one in those years when they drifted apart. June began to flick through them, most of them saying just "Love, Matt," but further down the pile, the messages were longer, and he called her "Little Sis." Near the bottom of the box, there was one with a lot of writing in it. She pulled it out, opened it, and read:

"Darling Little Sis, I know this will be a difficult Christmas for you. I am so sad for you. Let's hope 1946 is a better year than this one, that Dad will come round, and you'll find some happiness again. Ever your loving brother, Matt."

She read the words again, looking at the date. *1945—the year the Second World War ended. A lot of people must have been hoping the next year would be better, but why was he so sad for her?* June put the card back on top of the pile and looked over to where Cathy was gingerly taking a fragile letter out of its envelope. From where June was, she could see that the envelope was addressed to Mr and Mrs S. Harrison, her grandparents.

Cathy was staring at the address at the top of the letter. It felt like minutes, but in a few seconds, she had opened the letter. "It's from Wales," was all she told June. "Wales."

Who was writing from Wales? wondered June, just before realisation spread across her puzzled face. "That's where Ed said Mum spent some time, isn't it? He seemed to imply that she had done something wrong. We know she had a baby. He was born in Wales, wasn't he? Read it, Cathy! Read it!"

Cathy could feel her hands shaking. It felt wrong, this invasion into her mother's past, and yet, the past was the key to finding out about the present—and they had to find out. It felt as if this was a different person, someone young that they'd never known.

"Dear Mummy and Daddy,

I am writing to let you know that I have arrived safely at Auntie Betty's cottage. I was met at the station, as arranged, and the train from London was on time. Auntie Betty is very kind, and I am sure I will be well looked after. I shall, of course, do all I can to help her while I am here, as there is a lot to do. She has chickens that lay eggs every morning, and she has some sheep in a field behind the cottage. It has been very wet here since I arrived, but I am hoping it will soon dry up, so that I can see the hills in some sunshine and walk to the village.

I hope you are both well. Perhaps you will be able to visit me in a few weeks?

Love,

Maggie

There were two more letters, bound together with a piece of string, in the same large, brown envelope that had held the first, labelled simply "M." Both were from Maggie to her parents. One described her daily routine and the shops in the village, and again inquired as to whether they would visit. The other was obviously written sometime later.

"Dear Mummy and Daddy,

No doubt you will have heard from Auntie Betty by now, about the details of the last few days. I know she was able to make a telephone call from the post office to let you know that your grandson had been born. I don't know whether you would like to see him while he is here, but if you can't manage it, here is a photograph, which a kind neighbour took for us. He is already showing signs of being very fair, and he has beautiful blue eyes, which he can now open. I cannot help but love him, and I know that someone else will love him, too. My heart will break when I have to part with him, but I pray that life will be good to him and that someone will give him the happy childhood I cannot. I shall have to pray that God will grant me the strength I need to do what I know must be done.

Auntie Betty says I am doing quite well now, and I may soon be able to go out, as I seem to be regaining my colour. She has been so kind, and I shall be eternally grateful to her. Some of the women in the village have brought little knitted coats for him, which will, of course, go with him in a few weeks' time.

I hope you are both well.

Your daughter,

Maggie.

"Oh June, someone kept these letters she wrote, didn't they? Do you think it could have been her mother?"

"Could well have been, by the looks of it. Maybe Mum found them when her own mother died, because they've all been stored in that envelope with an M on the front, as if they were a secret stash. There don't seem to be any replies, though, do there? And it doesn't look as if they ever went to Wales, does it? They didn't see the baby, it seems."

"From the way Ed spoke to us, it was all hushed up, so she must have had to come back here and pretend it never happened," June said. "People will have whispered about why she'd been away, wouldn't they?"

"Bound to have done. What about the father? He doesn't seem to be mentioned, does he?"

"No. Let's keep looking."

Slowly, as if afraid they would be discovered plundering the contents, they began to sift through more shoe boxes inside the chest. Inside one was a collection of postcards, sent from all over the country at various times, presumably from friends and more distant family. On top, there were some intriguing old views of places June still knew, but underneath these some of them were similar to ones she'd recently seen in a museum when she'd taken the twins to see an exhibition of old postcards and magazines. There were the typical cartoon women with huge breasts and behinds, and men with cigarettes hanging out of the corner of their mouths. One depicted a man on the beach, a scantily clad woman in his arms, saying, "I must send a postcard to the missus, but I haven't got anything exciting to tell her," while the woman running down the beach with a club in her hand was, presumably, the missus.

"Can you imagine anyone finding that funny now?" June asked.

Cathy took a quick look and rolled her eyes, moving on to another postcard that would have had animal protection societies up in arms, as a huge woman sat on a small donkey and joked about the donkey being tired. "People could send these, yet mum was censored. What a joke."

June sighed. "The hypocrisy is unbearable."

Further down in the chest was an old tin that originally held toffees, with a beautiful country cottage painted on the lid. It looked as if it were from the 1950s. Cathy lifted it out carefully, though it took some strength to open it. It had obviously been shut for a long time. As the lid finally gave, it sprung out of her hand, and the contents flew into the chest.

June reached down to pick up a piece of blue ribbon and a tiny pair of knitted baby boots, while Cathy slowly lifted a small black and white photograph with a crinkly edge. It showed the head and shoulders of a young man in uniform with a dazzling smile—dark hair daring to show round the edges of his hat. She turned it over, and there was a date stamp on the back: January 1944. In ink was handwritten, "To MH with love from WE," and in a different handwriting "Bill."

Cathy placed it carefully back in the tin as she gathered up another, slightly larger, black, and white photograph of a baby wrapped in a shawl that had ribbon threaded round the edge. All that was visible of the baby was its face, its eyes peering as if it could not yet see clearly. It lay in what looked like a drawer. Hoping to find a clue on the back again, Cathy turned it over carefully, as it seemed more fragile than the first photograph from being handled repeatedly. The flip side was blank, however, no clues whatsoever.

She set it down on the lid of the tin, so June could see it as clearly as she could. Neither of them uttered a word. It suddenly felt as if to do so would be like whispering in church when everyone was supposed to be praying. On their knees, they looked from one photograph to the other, knowing that this baby was neither of them.

At last, June said, "It's him, isn't it? Our brother. And maybe W.E. is his father."

"Looks like it," answered Cathy, weakly. For some reason, she was welling up with tears, though he meant nothing to her. It took her a moment, but she realised it was for her mother that she cried. Her mother who had kept this hidden, precious tin all those years and must have come up here sometimes, just to see her baby's face again. How cruel it seemed today, that she had loved and lost not just the man but his baby, too. In those days of no welfare state, no benefits or support, only shame, she had born the consequences of their relationship alone, and no one had let her keep the baby she'd carried.

A sense of the grief Maggie must have had to bury inside was overwhelming to her daughters, so that all they could do was pass the items back and forth, staring at the smiling face of the handsome airman. They found some pieces of paper folded in the bottom of the tin, seemingly a contract for adoption. They could only imagine how it had felt to sign confirmation that she was surrendering him. Later, perhaps they should pass on the papers to the solicitor, in case they helped in tracing him and fulfilling their mother's wishes, but for now, they just put everything back into the tin and replaced it in the chest.

As they sat back on their heels, they both knew it was time to abandon their search. They wordlessly worked together to leave the contents of the chest as they had found them, shut the lid, and clambered back out of the loft. As June was dusting off her hands, she heard laughter, chatter, and barking dogs followed by the slamming of the back door.

PART FIVE

"We should always allow some time to elapse, for time discloses the truth."

- Seneca

Chapter Twenty-One

Standing on the cliff top, looking out at Bedruthan Steps, Vicky wondered how her mother could have borne leaving such a beautiful place. The turquoise sea rose rhythmically over the rocks, like a comforting lullaby, as the spring sun glistened like silver on the waves. She'd been to Cornwall before, of course, but in her childhood days, when her grandfather had been very elderly. She'd always thought of him as her grandfather; there had never been any question of thinking of him any differently because her mother was adopted. They were who they were; as far as she and Mike had been concerned, Bronwyn and David were Caroline's doting parents who lived at the seaside and always seemed so pleased to see them. That was enough. For some reason no one ever explained, Caroline had never shown them as much affection as they'd shown her, but Vicky and Mike had only ever known them to be indulgent and affectionate.

There weren't enough bedrooms for all of them, so they'd made their visits when they were staying down there, but they never actually stayed in the cottage itself. Vicky tried hard to remember what it looked like, but she doubted that she could find it without her father's help. She walked back to where her father sat, drinking a cup of tea, and showing Georgie the wrist action he needed to skim pebbles on the beach. The wind blew strands of his grey hair into his eyes, and she shuddered as she saw him getting old in the way his hands moved with difficulty and his back was beginning to bow. Time was cruel, snatching from under your nose what you thought you were, what you thought others were. Her dad—her rock—was slowly turning into more granddad than dad.

Bob had done well since his accident, and he was almost back to the person he'd been before, but she couldn't turn back the clock. There was no recovery from time chipping away a bit of memory here, a bit of sight there, a bit of hearing. He never complained, but Vicky wanted to shout from the cliff top for him: "Leave me alone, Time! Go wear away some rocks instead!"

They'd driven down to St Eval before lunch, to see where David was stationed during the war. He'd fallen in love with Cornwall and Bronwyn, who'd been one of the women serving there as well. Vicky had seen a creased and faded photograph of them on the day they were engaged—both in uniform—kept in a brown tin in David's bureau along with a collection of other photos. Some were tiny with crinkled edges, all black and white or sepia, and turning brown with age. She and Mike had been fascinated by them on the rare occasions when David had taken them out of the tin to tell the stories behind them. It had been one of their favourite parts of their visits.

They'd found it impossible to think of the old couple as once so young and handsome, and looking so much in love. David would tell them how it was taken by one of his crew the week before he was shot down. There was a photograph of their wedding at the end of the war, so faded it was impossible to see who stood behind them in the church doorway, but David told the children they'd gone back to St Eval to be married. With part of the runway still intact, it had been easy to imagine them in that place, and Bob had been visibly moved as he looked at the dedications to the men and women who had served there.

What must it have been like, Vicky wondered, *to have faced that daily danger, never to know whether the one you love would still be there at the end of the day*? Their love must have been a desperate grasping of what they could have at that time, whatever the future held, however short it was. They could only live for today, but maybe they planned for tomorrow. She thought of the old wartime songs she'd heard so often with a dispassionate lack of understanding. They must have had to cling to that hope that the white cliffs of Dover would be free, and that they would meet again in the face of the bombs and the dogfights and the horror of enemy fire.

David and Bronwyn had settled in Cornwall in 1950. Vicky knew her mother had arrived in 1952, and although she never had any siblings, she'd grown up in a safe, close community with freedoms Vicky would never have dared let Georgie have. She'd left to go to university, the first in her family to do so, and she never went back to live at home.

Staring at her father and her son, she felt a deep gratitude for that generation and relief that her father hadn't had to fight like that. He didn't say much about his time in the navy, other than tales of where he'd been, what he'd seen, and who and what he knew. He seemed to have enjoyed his times at sea, but she knew there were probably things he would never tell her. He seemed to know people all over the country and beyond, and he would tell his tales to anyone who would listen. She smiled to herself as she remembered how her mother had raised her eyebrows as he amused a new audience with exploits she'd heard many times before. He was never happier than when he was in company.

"OK, folks. Shall we wend our way to Padstow now?"

"Mum, can we go on the ferry you talked about? Can we?" Georgie was growing up fast, but his boyish enthusiasm jolted Vicky from her thoughts and grounded her in the moment.

She smiled at him. "Well, we'll have to see whether it's running, and what time, but yes, if it's possible. Uncle Mike and I used to love it!"

They set off as the sun streaked through lambs' wool clouds curling round the sky. As they drove towards Padstow, Georgie disappeared into his own world, headphones delivering what her radio did not. Bob sat beside her, staring out across the fields, and she wondered what memories of his wife's past he held in his thoughts. It felt as if she would be intruding to ask, so she kept her eyes on the road ahead. Three people, each locked into their own thoughts, and not daring to invade each other's reality.

Suddenly, Bob startled her with, "Turn left, Vicky, just down there! Turn left!"

Without time to ask why, Vicky indicated and swung the car round into a lane that seemed too narrow for comfort.

"Where are we going, Dad?" she asked nervously.

"Just keep going, Vicky. It's down here."

"What's down here?"

Faced with a delivery van coming towards her round the bend, she slammed on the brakes, nearly sending her father through the windscreen. The van stopped a few yards in front of her, and she knew they couldn't possibly get past each other here. She searched in the rear mirror, and to her relief she found there was the gateway she'd just passed. Slamming the car into reverse, she prayed she would be able to drive backwards in a straight line, knowing full well that if she didn't, she would fulfil the prophecy of a woman driver being incapable. Slowly, she balanced the clutch and accelerator and steered them back into the gateway, the van advancing as she reversed, impatient to be on its way.

Vicky was about to vent her frustration, demanding why her father had taken her down this ridiculous lane, when as she rounded the bend, she saw it, and he was instantly forgiven. Bright-white render peeked through the hedgerow, and a familiar silver birch tree towered over the distinctive chimney. As they approached the large, iron gates, which always seemed out of proportion for the size of the cottage, the road widened, and they were able to pull into a space on the opposite side of the road. Beyond the gates, the palm tree she remembered being planted on her mother's birthday still stood in the middle of a circular flower bed, now resplendent with colour. Someone obviously loved this place as much as her grandparents had. When they died it was sold, and her mother used her share of the proceeds to renovate and extend their house. Vicky had been too young to take any interest, and money was not openly discussed in front of the family. She had no idea who bought the cottage, but it was somehow satisfying to see it cared for. She had happy memories of skipping in the garden and swaying on the rope swing that hung from a huge horse chestnut, jumping off in mid-air, to see who could land furthest from it. Mike had always won, but she'd got close. As a child, she remembered the garden rambling for what felt like miles down to an orchard where they could pick their own apples.

A huge greenhouse housed her grandfather's precious cuttings and tomatoes, and there always seemed to be something he was growing. He would take his grandchildren into the warm, humid atmosphere of his heated area and explain to them how to look after the peppers or pansies, or whatever he was growing. Grandma had moaned about the time he spent on his plants, saying that he cared more about them than he did about anything else, but to Mike and Vicky he seemed like an eccentric teacher; he was full of fascinating facts, and he let them get their hands dirty, much to their grandmother's disgust.

It seemed to Vicky that her grandparents didn't like each other much, yet when her grandmother died, her grandfather had pined away, and within months he was gone too.

Vicky wondered whether the greenhouse was still standing, and whether anyone grew anything with the same care as her grandfather. *Does the swing still hang from the branch? Are someone else's children flying as high as they could, glimpsing over the hedgerow and spying on the garden next door?*

"Shall we get out and have a look?" Her father's voice broke into her reverie, like someone waking her up in the morning before she was ready. Slowly, her brain focused on his question, which hung in the air while Georgie heard nothing but the music through his headphones.

"Oh... er... do you think they'd mind?"

"Well, it can't hurt to peer through the gates, can it?" Bob insisted.

Tapping Georgie on the shoulder, Vicky mouthed that they were getting out of the car. He pulled a face, reluctantly clambering off the back seat and following them across the road. Like prisoners looking out through the bars, the three of them leant into the ironwork, trying to see as much as possible.

"What are we doing here?" asked Georgie, wondering why they were being so nosy. He felt a little on edge, as if someone might suddenly let a dog loose on them.

"This is where Grannie's parents lived, Georgie, when I was a little girl. Uncle Mike and I used to play over there, and behind the house." Vicky was gesturing excitedly. "Oh, and look! See that statue over there? That was nearly as big as me! It looks as if they have the same front door, but the windows have been changed, haven't they?" she commented, turning to her father.

Bob just managed to agree before a voice with a strange accent came out of the air, and it took a few seconds for them to locate it to the intercom on the wall.

"Can I help you?" the voice asked. "Why are you staring through my gates?"

Blushing, Vicky gathered her wits as quickly as she could. "I'm so sorry to have disturbed you. We were just passing, and we recognised the cottage as the one where my mother's parents used to live. It was just nostalgia that made us look. I do apologise if we have invaded your privacy. We'll go now."

"Wait," said the disembodied voice. "Stay there! I'm coming out."

The front door opened with a creak, and a man Vicky thought probably in his seventies emerged. He wore a kindly smile, leaned heavily on a walking stick, and shuffled in his tweed slippers across the gravel drive. The gates seemed to slowly open of their own accord as he called to the three interlopers. "Come into the garden, will you? It will save me walking all the way down the drive."

The trio did as they were asked, reassured by his twinkling eyes and the gentle, elegant insistence of his free hand. As they met halfway down the drive, he seemed to look them up and down before deciding what to say. He turned to Vicky, as spokesperson, but gave a nod to Bob. The latter was fiddling with the change in his pocket, wondering whether they should have just driven on. After his last experience of tracking down the past, Bob doubted the wisdom of doing it again.

"So, who did you say used to live here, then?" the elderly householder asked.

"My mother's parents. We used to come here when I was a small child. This is my father, Bob Thompson. I am Vicky Thompson, and this is my son, George.

"Thompson, you say." His forehead crinkled as he ruminated. "So, who was your mother, then? Who were your grandparents?"

Hesitating, Vicky wondered about the safety of revealing names to this stranger who was very obviously not even English. Australian, she guessed from the intonation. "My mother was Caroline Hitchen before she was married. My grandparents were Bronwyn and David Hitchen."

"I think you'd better come in," said the old gentleman. "I wondered when one of you would turn up."

They followed him into the hall, which seemed smaller than Vicky remembered, though the sunlight shone through the stained-glass panel, just as it did in her memory. He led them into the lounge, where two large sofas faced each other on either side of an enormous fireplace. He invited them to sit down, and all three perched awkwardly on the same sofa while he sat opposite them, his stick between his legs, and both of his hands carefully folded over the handle. He pensively ran his fingers over his grey beard, and Vicky could discern a slight trembling of his leg as he weighed up what to say.

"I met Caroline once," he began, claiming their attention. "I think it was back in the 1950s, when I was on leave. I worked abroad, you see."

Bob and Vicky were still trying to compute what he had just said, when he continued, "She was a little girl, of course, and that was before she went away to school. I never got the chance to get to know her, as I lived too far away, and I became estranged from my parents."

"How did you come to meet her, then, may I ask?" ventured Vicky, wondering what his parents had to do with anything.

"You don't know, do you?" He looked at her, then at Bob, staring straight into their eyes, as if searching for something.

"It would seem we don't know what we don't know," answered Bob, with a smile on his face. "I think you'd better explain, if you don't mind."

"You say your grandparents were Bronwyn and David?"

"Yes," Vicky said with a nod.

"But your mother—your wife, I assume, sir—was Caroline?"

"Yes," Bob chimed in.

"But you see, that isn't quite right."

Georgie was fidgeting, bored with this conversation between adults. *What on earth are they doing, sitting in this boring room, talking to a boring old man?* he thought. He wanted to be doing something, anything that meant getting out of here.

"Young man, why don't you go and explore the garden?" The old man said, as if reading his mind. In reality, he'd spotted Georgie's twitchy legs and twirly fingers. He smiled kindly through his grey-and-white moustache, his eyes lighting as if he were up to mischief.

Georgie was startled, his voice having disappeared somewhere in the back of his throat. He looked at Vicky, his eyes pleading with her to let him go.

"Go out of here, turn left, and follow the corridor down to the kitchen," directed the man. "You'll find the back door unlocked."

Vicky nodded her approval. "Sure, Georgie. Go see what you can find. Give it five minutes or so. Wipe your feet when you come back in, won't you?"

Already rising and not needing to be told twice, Georgie bolted through the doorway and headed in the direction of the kitchen, leaving Vicky and Bob to gather their thoughts.

"So why isn't it right?" Bob was not about to give this stranger any additional information. He wanted to know what the old man knew. "You said it wasn't right."

"She wasn't actually their daughter, was she?" the man asked. "You knew that?"

Vicky was remembering the half-buried fact that she knew her mother had been adopted by Bronwyn and David, but she wondered what was coming next.

"Yes, we knew that," Bob replied. "They adopted her as a baby. Her mother died."

"She was their granddaughter. Did you realise that? Her mother was my father's younger sister, Penny. My name is Thomas David Hitchen."

The silence hung in the air between them as Bob and Vicky assimilated the facts. "So how come we never knew you existed, then?" Vicky launched at him, doubting his story, and wondering what kind of game he was playing.

"My father's sister married and moved away, and my father emigrated to Australia," Thomas began. "I didn't get along with my grandparents, as they never forgave me for a lifestyle they considered to be wrong. You see, my partner was male at a time when to live as a couple was illegal. In their eyes, I am a fallen man, worse than a fallen woman, and they disowned me. As you probably know, they were very religious, and the rules were black and white to them. I was a disgrace, bordering on evil in their eyes. They were good people, but they couldn't cope with who I was, once it came to light. I lost touch with my aunt, who couldn't be tainted with my sins, and I doubt that she even knew I still existed. When we dared to come back for a visit, to find our

English family, we discovered that she'd died and Caroline, her child, was being brought up in the same suffocating atmosphere that my father had escaped. She must have been glad to go away to school!"

"They were good grandparents," said Vicky, feeling as if she had to spring to the defence of the memories she held dear. "Grandma was a bit strict, but they made us welcome, and she baked us cakes while Grandpa showed us his plants."

"Ah yes, the plants. He loved them, whatever kind of deviant they turned out to be!" uttered Thomas, with a bitter laugh. "I'm glad you managed to enjoy yourselves here. As a child, I loved it, too."

"So, you are my mother's cousin, then?" The thought dawned on Vicky, as she made sense of what she was hearing.

"And you live here now?" asked Bob, wondering why someone who had been brought up in Australia was living in his wife's parents' house.

"Ah, no. I'm afraid my home is on the other side of the world. The house was sold, when my grandparents died, as you must know. It was my father who arranged to buy it, reclaiming his childhood home, so that he could come back to visit it whenever he wanted to. It's been let out for a long time, but my brother and I are getting too old to hang on to it much longer, and I'm here to settle the last of my father's affairs. He lived until he was ninety-seven, you see, so when he left half of this to me, it seemed like a good idea to keep it for a while. But that was my heart ruling my head, and now my head must rule my heart. It's time to pick out some of the precious things that might be worth transporting across the world and to sell the rest."

"We arrived just in time to see it as it is, then?" mused Bob.

"You sure did. Did you say your name was Vicky?"

"Yes." Vicky nodded, reciprocating his smile.

"Well, if you've got anything that can prove your identity to me, would you like to have a look round and see whether there's something you'd like to take with you as a keepsake for your mother?"

"That's so kind. I don't know what to say, but maybe there's a photo or something that I can pass on to my son." Vicky searched her handbag for identification. "Look, here's my driving licence." She held it out in front of Thomas, realising that the surname wasn't the same.

Thomas was being very trusting, however, and with a cursory nod said, "Of course. Have a wander round and bring back what you think might be good to have. I'll go and make a cup of tea while you and your dad take a tour." Then he passed her and padded down the corridor to the kitchen.

The tour didn't take long, but Bob found the nostalgic walk around the house quite difficult at first. He remembered the grandfather clock striking the hour, though it was now silent. He recalled how David had been a collector of anything that took his interest, so he wasn't surprised to see the clutter that had been hidden from them, and presumably from anyone who'd rented the house. Thomas had obviously been busy clearing out the cupboards in the eaves that flanked the bedroom at the top of the house. They'd rarely been upstairs, since they'd always stayed elsewhere over night, but the ornaments, lamps, and framed prints of old masters were just as they had been years ago, and he welled up as he thought about how they had been someone's precious possessions and now meant nothing to those that looked at them.

In the dining room, just to the side of the fireplace, Vicky's eye was caught by some old photos. They were ranged on an embroidered cloth atop an old table with barley-twist legs. She had no idea who most of them were, but it seemed important to save them from obscurity. She gathered them up before continuing through the rest of the house.

Ten minutes later, when Vicky and Bob re-entered the lounge, Thomas was busy showing Georgie a collection of old motorcycle magazines he'd found stowed away in a cupboard. It seemed they shared a passion for the fast and dangerous, just as her brother did.

"You found something, then?" asked Thomas, looking at Vicky's clutch of silver frames.

"Yes. If you don't mind, I'd like to keep the photos in case I can identify who they are," she answered.

As he poured the tea, gesturing his question about taking sugar or not, Thomas offered, "Fine. I can probably help you with some of that. This one," he said, pointing, "is Bronwyn and David when they'd just got engaged. It's the official, stiff photograph. They didn't seem to be told to smile in those days! This one is Penny—my dad had the same photo—with her husband, I think. I seem to remember that his name was Mitchell. He looks a handsome devil, doesn't he, with his hair falling over his face? Ah—now this one is my dad. Again, he had the same photo. I think it's the last one he had taken before he emigrated." Thomas paused as he took the last photograph in the pile and seemed to study it, a frown edging over his brow. "Well, well," he said. "I would never have thought they'd have kept a photo of me! This is me when I graduated. A long time ago now."

Vicky looked at the portrait of a young man with brown hair, not grey, no moustache or beard. His young, clean-shaven face reminded her of Mike. He sat gracefully, his hands posed carefully and one leg in front of the other. He was strikingly handsome. "Would you like that one yourself?" she asked. "Maybe they didn't cast you off, after all, you know. They kept your photo."

"They kept the image they wanted," Thomas retorted. "No. I have plenty of photos of myself. You are welcome to it if you want it."

As they finished their tea, Vicky rounded up her photographs and persuaded Georgie to leave the magazines behind. It was only after they left that she realised they hadn't exchanged addresses, and she had no idea how to contact Thomas again.

They climbed back into the car, and she felt like Judy Garland in *The Wizard of Oz*, as if it would all turn out to be unreal. If her father and Georgie weren't with her, she would have been tempted to think she'd dreamt the whole thing. How astonishing that she had a relative she'd never known about, that her grandparents were her great-grandparents, and that her mother had an uncle she had never mentioned. She needed to try to start making sense of all of this.

Chapter Twenty-Two

Libby had forgotten about the DNA test results. Now, sitting on the train to London with her friend Annabelle, she was bored enough to sort through her emails, looking again at those she'd flagged to revisit when she had time. There it was, the notification that she could view her results. They were stored somewhere on her tablet, if she could remember what she'd called the file.

Wouldn't it be great if I discovered a long lost, very rich relative, who could spoil me like Belle's father spoils her? she thought. *Fat chance! If only my dad had worked in finance in the city. If only my dad had stuck around.*

"Do you remember doing this, Belle?" Libby asked her friend.

"Oh yes! Did you ever do anything with them? Did you find your red-headed ancestors?"

"No. Things were hectic at uni and miserable at home, so I wasn't in the right frame of mind. I doubt that they tell me anything I don't already know."

"Well, if you don't look, you won't know, will you? Why don't we have a look now? Go on, I dare you! You might be related to someone famous. Someone I know found they were a distant cousin of a member of the Rolling Stones!" Annabelle goaded her with a grin.

"Oh, OK. I'll pull up what they sent me," Libby agreed.

Curiosity drew her towards the results now. Nothing unexpected about the pie chart and stats she skimmed over. Surprise, surprise, she was mostly well and truly British, with a smattering of Scandinavian and a bit of French. She threw back her head with a derisory laugh. "Well, there you go, then! Vikings and Normans invaded my ancestors with their gene pool!"

Libby decided to log in to see what other information might be there, expecting nothing of any consequence, but she didn't have anything else to do for the next two hours, so in for a penny, in for a pound.

It seemed the test threw up people she might be related to. She wouldn't risk contacting anyone, but it was interesting to see who might be out there carrying similar DNA. As the two girls peered at the lists, it became clear that Libby seemed to have distant relatives across the country, from Kent and London—not just in the north, where she might have expected them.

Someone called Victoria was listed as a possible close cousin, but that couldn't be right. Surely, she would know about someone like that. The list of contenders meant nothing without a family tree, she decided, and as far as she knew, no one had bothered to do one.

Maybe she'd ask her mum when she got home for Easter. She might know some of it. She could make a start with her own information and others she could name, but it didn't go far. She could remember one side of her mother's grandparents' names, but she'd never been interested enough to ask about others, and it wasn't something her family had ever discussed. Now was not the time to quiz her mother, so she'd see what she could find out herself.

"I'll leave you to it," Belle declared, sinking behind her thick book.

Apprehensively, Libby pulled up the genealogy web site. Where to begin? She soon realised that anything recent wouldn't be there, so the only way to go was to search for births.

She wasn't sure how long her fingers hovered over the screen, but when she glanced sideways, she saw that Belle had fallen asleep against the window, her book resting on the table between them.

It was going to be tricky doing this on a train, as she knew the signal would disappear as soon as she went into a tunnel. She knew she could try signing into the train company's Wi-Fi, but that had been singularly unsuccessful in the past, and it didn't seem worth the effort. She typed her grandmother's name into the search, and there was an unexpected feeling of excitement as the screen was suddenly full of people with the surname Harrison, more than one of them Margaret. Next she tried Mitchell, and there were both a Phillip and a Samuel.

Infuriatingly, there were no dates to be seen, unless she paid, but what she was finding was enough to draw her in, make her want to know more, and she wished she could save what was on the screen. She took a screen shot of two pages, deciding she needed to know more about how to follow the trail of these snippets of information. She turned her attention to searching for websites that could be useful, making a list of favourites to come back to later. By the time Belle woke up, Libby had decided that she'd be spending part of her Easter holiday pulling this together.

"Good morning," joked Libby, as Belle stretched and yawned, just as the train approached the station. "You have got the tickets for the show, haven't you?"

"Of course, I have, silly! I intend to enjoy my birthday treat!" Belle reached for her bag, pulling out the paper wallet and waving it in front of Libby's face. "See! Safe and sound!"

"What a stroke of luck that your dad's friend had spares! I feel so lucky! Of course, you could have asked Declan to come with you," she teased, knowing that Belle's father knew nothing of his daughter's love life.

"Dad's hardly going to let me stay in the London apartment with a boy, is he? Anyway, Declan and I are just good friends." Her laughter held a hint of something more.

"Well, I hope I'm your best friend then," chuckled Libby.

Libby managed not to utter the "Wow!" that was inside her head when they arrived at the apartment, and Belle let them in with the key her uncle allowed her to keep. The apartment was obviously once part of a warehouse, but now it was the complete opposite of her mother's slightly shabby, comfortable but cluttered home. Everything seemed to shine, from metal lampshades dangling from vaulted ceilings, to gleaming black worktops and glossy white units. Nothing seemed to be out of place; it was as though no one lived there at all. There wasn't even a kettle because boiling water came out of a tap.

Libby couldn't imagine anyone daring to walk on the fluffy white rug that sat in the centre of the room, and almost the whole of one wall was glass, with a Juliet balcony offering a view of the river she'd never had before. From five floors up, she could watch the busy thoroughfare. Everyone seemed to be rushing somewhere, but the bustling activity excited her.

Belle pulled her friend away from the window and insisted they take their bags up to the mezzanine floor. As they climbed the open treads of the glass-sided staircase, Libby greedily digested what she could see below. *One day*, Libby thought, *I'll have one of these*. She felt as if she were in an unreal world, where she couldn't even have dreamt this apartment. The sense of being someone else pervaded the whole evening, even when they were returning in a cab, singing "Circle of Life" in the back seat.

The following morning, Libby heard the entrance door glide to a close and the rattle of keys. She looked over at Belle, who was curled up on a separate futon a few feet away. If she called her name, whoever it was in the lounge would hear, since they were on what her mother would call the landing. Just as she was considering edging across the floor to tap her friend's foot, a voice called from below.

"Annabelle! Are you there?"

She heard her friend stir and mutter in a sleepy voice, "Hi, Dad. Give me a few minutes, and we'll come down."

After a scramble for the shower room and clothes, the two girls began descending. From behind the huge cream sofa, Libby saw a head of raven-black hair and a man probably in his thirties, as neat and tidy as the apartment, but still wearing his expensive leather shoes and his jacket as if he were not there to stay. He was obviously listening to music through his Bluetooth earbuds, so he didn't hear them approaching.

Belle moved faster as she got to the bottom of the stairs, going around the sofa and abruptly facing him, her hands on her hips. "Oh! You're not my dad! Who are you? How did you get in here?"

As he smiled, he removed the earbuds and stood up. "Ah—you must be Annabelle! Your father asked me to pop in to make sure everything was OK. I don't know whether he was more worried about whether you would get here safely or whether you would wreck the joint with a party he hadn't sanctioned. Both you and the apartment, it seems, are rather precious."

"Well, here we are, as you can see. And we are perfectly responsible, thank you. So, who are you, how do you know my father, and how do you have a key?"

"Have you checked your phone? You should have a message explaining that I'm Mike, the son of one of your father's friends. They go way back, apparently." The man smiled in an effort to diffuse the situation, but when Belle's fists didn't move from her hips, he went on, "I was introduced to your father when I was a child. He and Dad used to meet up in town, until Dad had his accident. He put me up here for a few days when I first came to London. He knows I work in town, so he lent me a key and asked me to check up on things for him."

Belle reached for her phone, wondering how she had missed a text. Nothing. Slowly, she realised her father would not automatically text her, and as she pulled up her email instead, there it was:

You remember my old pal from my navy days? His son, Mike, will drop in to make sure everything is OK. Don't worry if you're out—he has a key. If you need help with anything, he's your man. Take care. Love, Dad.

Belle glanced up to find Mike waiting for her response. He rocked on his heels impatiently. "So, was the show good?"

Belle didn't thaw quite that easily, and she eyed him with suspicion that cooled his warm smile. "It was excellent, thank you. You don't need to babysit us."

Libby hung back, allowing her friend to take the lead since this was her father's domain. She liked what she saw, and she wondered how Belle was managing to stay so severe. *This Mike is drop-dead gorgeous*, she thought, immediately scolding herself for even thinking that expression. From the tip of his head to the sole of his shoes, all six feet of him oozed confidence and charm. Not a hair out of place, he looked as if he should be modelling for a high-class fashion magazine. *I can just imagine what a camera would make of those blue eyes against his olive skin!* Libby thought. The cut of his jacket, the casual but somehow smart shirt, and the shine on his shoes would not look out of place in a photo-shoot or a film, and even his jeans seemed to fit with a perfection that her bargain-store student outfit could never hope to match.

Mike held out his hand to shake Belle's, and she reluctantly took it. "Look, I'm glad you're OK. I'll give your dad a ring and let him know.

Enjoy your day in London. If you do have any problems, I'm at your service. Mike Thompson. Here's my business card. You'll find my mobile number on there. Right, I'll leave you two ladies to get your breakfast and find your way to the tourist traps. Bye for now. Nice to meet you."

He turned crisply towards the door and quietly exited the room.

"Creepy, or what?" said Belle.

"Oh, I thought he was rather nice," answered Libby. "It was good of him to make sure we're OK."

"He probably owes my dad a favour," snapped Belle. "Come on. Let's get some breakfast. I'm starving. We'll go to Greggs."

Chapter Twenty-Three

Cathy strode up the hill towards Wickham Hall, head bowed and hands in her pockets, not entirely sure why she was doing this. The daffodils waved their heads in the breeze and crocuses pushed up through the grass verges, their colours claiming spring as theirs. She noticed the birds beginning to flock across the fields, and the world around her seemed to be bursting into new life while her consciousness was firmly held in an old life she struggled to reclaim. The past called to her, beckoning her onto the top of the hill.

As the Hall came into view, she imagined her father standing at the gate, his lopsided ready smile waiting for her as she ran to meet him after school—fair hair falling over his eyes as it always did, however much he tried to tame it. Somehow, he'd always made her feel safe. She pictured his large, work-worn hands, so capable and warm, waiting to lift her up and toss her in the air as if she were as light as a feather. Her laughter had been pure joy.

She and June had taken turns to ride on the crossbar of his bicycle, whizzing down the hill, ringing the bell as they zoomed into the yard. How she wished she could recapture that feeling of abandon! She longed to hear his comforting voice telling her everything was going to be all right. She wanted to believe that again, but somehow the gnawing feeling in her stomach would not be convinced. It seemed as if life just kept throwing the unexpected at her, like someone aiming at a coconut shy in a fairground, the prize being the removal of her peace of mind.

Was it her own fault? Did she just hand it over? She was no longer sure whether fate or her own actions had been the root of her situation, but failure was the outcome she felt. Here was June, her children around her, her job satisfying her, contentment oozing from her. Why didn't she feel that same satisfaction with her life? Others wowed at her photographs that captured a lifestyle most of them could only dream of. She'd made it to the top, despite the odds. She had a beautiful home full of beautiful things, remaining pristine and undisturbed by the turmoil of invasion by the young. Yet here she was, wishing that somehow she could capture that feeling of home. She was reeling from the discoveries she and June made in the loft. It was as if her mother had a secret life, of which they were not a part. Under the surface of the woman they'd thought they knew was someone else, someone not shared with them — a stranger. Had her father been who they thought he was, or had he also been someone else? How much of what she thought was her solid foundation was like quicksand instead, sinking away into a place she couldn't reach? What she thought she left, and could reclaim whenever she wished to, was becoming an illusion.

The past was being rewritten, and she no longer trusted it. It seemed it could acquire a life of its own, turning, chameleon-like, into something that camouflaged itself.

As Cathy stepped through the door, she felt the deep pile of the carpet below her feet and remembered how her small shoes would seem to sink into it, how she had loved to stroke the velvet door curtain as she passed. There it was, still held in its iron clip. On the wall ahead, the eyes of the stags' heads still seemed to follow her, as if they told her she'd better behave—or else. In the corner, the old suit of armour still stood proudly on guard, though she thought she detected a slight change in angle from when she was last here.

That thing still makes me feel as if someone might be inside it! she thought.

To her left rose the grand staircase she and her sister had loved to run up and down while they waited for their father to gather his possessions at the end of a day, and she remembered pretending to make a grand entrance, like a debutante, in her early teens.

The family crest still graced the glass on the half-landing, and in the fireplace to the right the coals burned a welcome as she moved forward into what had been a majestic hallway.

The family had never minded the girls coming to meet their father, and they'd been treated as an extension of the staff. She remembered the dowager, dressed completely in black, who would appear with her walking stick and give them sweets. Her mother had always disapproved, tutting about their teeth and people with more money than sense, which had made the sweets taste just that little bit better—a precious secret, unless their father had told on them.

If he didn't see, with a wink, the old lady would say, "Quick! Hide them in your pocket. Don't tell your father!"

As they grew older, they heard how she had lost two sons in the war and she loved children. When she died, the inheritance tax and the cost of buildings falling into disrepair stripped her son of what her family had owned for generations. Cathy knew that, in some ways, it had been a sad passing, though the privilege they enjoyed had been denied to so many. Her father had loved his job, as had others who worked there, but what they earned was no more than was considered appropriate to their station in life. It wouldn't be tolerated now.

As Cathy reached the newly installed reception desk, a young woman dressed in a plum-coloured suit came towards her with a walk that commanded respect—head held high and hair in a bun, looking like cabin crew on a prestigious airline. Her name badge said she was called Felicity, and she had striking green eyes. Her smile was placed with practice as she held out her hand to shake Cathy's. "Good afternoon, madam. I am Miss Foster, the duty manager. How may we help you?"

"Good afternoon, Miss Foster. My name is Cathy Mitchell. I live in Australia these days, but I'm over here on a visit to my sister, as our mother has recently died. My father used to work here when we were young, and I have many fond memories of coming into the house and grounds. I just wondered if I could have a wander round, for old time's sake? Can I do that, please?"

"Oh, I see. Well, Mrs Mitchell..."

"Miss."

"Miss Mitchell, I'm afraid we cannot just let you loose in the house. You see, we have guests staying, and they have a right to know that their security, and that of their possessions, will not be compromised in any way. I am prepared to accompany you to the first floor, but I'm afraid there is no possibility of entering any of the guests' rooms. You may take a tour of the grounds, if you wish, as we have CCTV cameras, which enable us to monitor movement outside. I'm sure you will understand." Her smile widened, as her eyes narrowed, suspicion broadcast loud and clear.

"Thank you so much, Miss Foster," Cathy heard herself say, while her mind thought something far less polite. "I would appreciate you accompanying me to the first floor. My father was estate manager, you see."

"You will find the estate much improved, I'm sure," replied Miss Foster, seemingly unaware of the insult she was delivering in her smooth, controlled tone.

With this, Cathy found herself guided to the staircase, where Miss Foster briskly led the way up towards the landing with the poise of one accustomed to superiority. The old photographs of the family still graced the drop over the stairs, some of them additions since Cathy remembered seeing them. *Why*, she wondered, *have they bothered to keep them*? Presumably, this had a marketing advantage, drawing those who aspired to gentility into what they could imagine as the genuine home of landed gentry.

From the window at the end of the long corridor full of closed doors, Cathy caught sight of the fountains and formal beds. The old rose-garden fountain she and June had played around, deliberately soaking themselves on warm days, had disappeared. In its place was a modern sculpture flanked by jets that threw water a mere metre into the air before depositing it around the base.

Not nearly as much fun for children, Cathy thought, *and not nearly as precious as the history the old fountain had owned*.

She was allowed a short pause before Miss Foster made much of consulting her watch, and she knew her permission was at an end. As they descended, she knew Miss Foster could not see her imitating the model's walk she and her sister had acquired for their imagined presentation to society. She felt the old satisfaction of the secret act and imagined the old lady winking at her from the bottom of the staircase.

She took her leave of Miss Foster as they reached the desk, thanking her for her indulgence of an overseas visitor and wishing her a "g'day." She could feel herself acquiring a stronger Australian accent than she usually had, satisfying her need to undermine the stiff formality, and hiding her real self from someone who seemed not to care who she was.

As she turned the corner, towards the back of the hotel, she half expected her father to appear from between the trees, clutching his trug or his secateurs, ready to catch her up as she ran into his arms. It was the same, yet different, as if the past and present blended into one. The greenhouse had gone, but the mark along the brick wall still indicated where it had been. There was still a pergola running from the fishpond to the ha-ha. In her mind's eye, she could see the glorious blue of the wisteria that would hang just above her head. She remembered how she and June would jump, trying to touch the blooms, and how they'd been warned not to do the same to the laburnum. The old laundry and the upper floors were now a small conference centre, and as she walked back towards the house, she could hear the chatter of those released into the fresh air. How different the place looked, and yet how good to hear it full of life and voices.

As she approached the house from the far side, she spotted another fountain, this one having survived the "improvements," and she could feel herself grinning. Gloriously overly ornate, its homage to the Greek gods had always seemed quite magical, especially when their father told them the stories associated with them. The fountain sat against a high wall, built just to accommodate its frenzy of figures—Eros in the centre, trying to outdo his other self in Piccadilly.

Cathy strode towards it, hearing tales echoing in her memory of Icarus flying too close to the sun and angry gods causing thunderstorms. How she wished her father were here now. His gentle wisdom was just what she needed. She knew she had no right to miss him, but in the three months since her mother's death, how she wished she had a parent to talk to. She'd never confided in them the real reason she had run away to the other side of the world, and she'd left them thinking her ambition was all that mattered. What would they have said if they'd known why she escaped? Just as she had as a child, she sat on the side of the fountain, dipping her fingers in the water and absentmindedly letting it run across her hands. Eros had a lot to answer for.

She wandered through the rose garden, back towards the front of the building, remembering how she would love to run from one bush to another, following the trail of fragrance and colour that delighted her while her father carefully chose the blooms to take into the house to grace the sitting room. Gone were the shrubs that had wrapped themselves around the lawn, replaced by the overflow car park and a low brick wall. As she approached the gates, she felt the breaking of the spell, as if she were crossing a threshold between the past and the present, finally leaving the past in its place.

Cathy set off down the hill, feeling her dad behind her, waving her goodbye. She wished she could have talked to him all those years ago, made him understand why she had to run away. Her parents had no idea how bad the bullying was for so many years.

She could still hear the taunts. "Hey, Teacher's Pet, what's wrong with you today?"

"Little Missy No-mates, eh? I wonder why?" Tracy's talons dug into her arm as she tried to pass without looking at the threesome leaning on the walls of the corridor.

I mustn't cry. I mustn't cry. Just ignore it. Don't give her the satisfaction of knowing it hurts.

"Did we get everything right today, then?" Tracy's pale face was thrust forward, her dyed auburn hair brushing Cathy's cheeks like stinging nettles, while Cathy kept her eyes focused on the floor. "Tell you what. If you bring us in some nice, expensive chocolate tomorrow, I just might forget to tell the Head how you cheated in the exam when you let me copy your answers. Go and see that posh lady you know. She'll give you some!" One of them had held her arm up her back until she agreed to help in the exam, and they often waylaid her to get answers to assignments.

Raucous laughter rang in Cathy's ears as she pulled her arm away and scuttled on to her next lesson.

It had started with name-calling when she was about thirteen, after she made the mistake of sitting at the front of a new class and putting up her hand too many times.

"Goody two-shoes!"

"Swat!"

"Posh paws!"

"Bitch!"

"Teacher's Pet" became the favourite. Notes were passed in class, reaching her anonymously. Whispers stopped as she got close to groups of girls. She was often left out of invitations at the weekends, and nobody picked her for their team, despite her love of netball.

In the playground, Cathy would be jostled. "Oh sorry! I didn't see you there! Did I hurt you? I'm so sorry!" The mock words were always followed by laughter.

They got bored with the physical game, as they got older, but the malice was always there, and they gave her a new nickname as she started to tell them to leave her alone. "Here, Catty, Catty, how many boys have you been with this week? Got any new clothes to show us? Did you drop a few marks in science? How could you? How's your posh friend, then? Give us a good miaow, Catty!"

Cathy knew that if she told on them, they would find out, and it would be worse. She had learnt to survive by being single-minded and determined to succeed.

After going through school being mocked or ignored for being bright and driven, university was a blissful interlude in feeling that she didn't fit in. As an undergraduate she'd found herself for the first time among others who didn't fit the mould, weren't one of a crowd, and who were genuinely interested in learning as well as having a good time. She'd learnt to enjoy the whirlwind of social life, even if it meant that sometimes she didn't sleep much for days when work was due in. She'd got her degree and landed herself a job in London, excited to throw herself into living and working in the capital.

People expected bullying to be something that happened at school—and that had been bad enough—but for Cathy it hadn't stopped there, and she became the object of the wrong kind of attention at work. She hadn't even recognised what was happening to her at first. When she'd looked around the offices, they were like something from a futuristic magazine and totally unlike anything at home. She thought it was a dream come true—but that was short-lived. It started with praise, which she lapped up, as it meant she was doing her job well, and her prospects were looking good.

"Hey, Cathy! You did a really good job there," her boss would say. "Could you pop into my office to discuss what you should do next? I think you could go far, young lady. It's a shame some of these others don't have the flair you've got. Brains and beauty—what a combination!"

She didn't notice that others in the office were also hearing the praise, and it was becoming obvious to them that her boss was making an example of her. There was a little innuendo in his banter, but she thought he was just a bit of a character, and she shrugged it off.

Then Cathy began to notice the same type of behaviour she had seen at school—conversation stopping as she passed, whispers ensuring she didn't hear what was said. People smiled at her, but they stopped including her when they went out to lunch.

Her boss began to comment on her appearance with a regularity that became uncomfortable. She began to notice that he called her into his office more often than her colleagues, but she hoped maybe this would mean she was marked out for rapid promotion.

"Well good morning, gorgeous!" he'd say, leaning over her shoulder at the copier. "I must say you look ravishing in that new outfit! You'll have the clients queueing up at the door! Come and brighten my day with your latest ideas!"

Morning coffee in his office became more frequent, and the comments on her work were punctuated with personal observations. "Love the perfume you're using, Cathy. What's that called?" He sniffed her hair, as he held the door open for her.

"I think it's just hairspray, actually, Don."

"Really? I thought it was all part of the cultivated allure," he joked. "You set a mighty strong honey trap for a man!"

He leant in close when he looked at her work, brushing up against her. She thought it was accidental, but then it became too close, too often.

He's a married man. He's got children. Maybe he just wants to be friendly, Cathy told herself. But when the touching started, she felt the alarm she didn't want to believe.

"We need to work very closely together, Cathy, if you're going to get the promotion you deserve." He laid his hand on her arm, squeezing it gently, making certain she could feel the unspoken implications.

Cathy thought she'd made friends in her first few weeks, but as the months passed, the friendships seemed to fade—apart from Anna, a few years older than her, who seemed to be watching what was happening with some concern. One afternoon, when Cathy had been in her boss's office for half an hour, dodging his body and deflecting his comments, it was Anna who saw her distress. She dropped what she was doing and made her way to Cathy. "Are you OK?"

"Fine, thanks," replied Cathy, her eyes on the papers she shuffled.

"You're not, are you?" probed Anna, her concern evident in her gentle tone. "Look, Cathy, I've seen it before. I know what's going on. You should report him, the creep."

"How can I? You know he'll just say it was innocent, and I'll end up out of a job."

"You shouldn't have to put up with it. You're good at your job. You're good looking and smart. That shouldn't mean you have to be a target for his lecherous attention." Anna looked over her shoulder, glancing at the boss's office before she said in a low tone, "He's done it to others. He collects women like medals, if they're daft enough to welcome him, then discards them for the next model. We've all seen it happening, and you don't welcome it, do you?"

"No, I don't. I just want to do my job." Cathy slapped down the paperwork a little harder than she intended. "I don't know what to do. This is my first job. I'll need a reference, and he's the one who will have to provide it, isn't he? Maybe if I just don't respond, he'll get the message that I'm not interested."

Anna made sympathetic noises, but she had no solutions. Cathy decided she'd stay long enough to get some experience on her CV, then look for another job. In hindsight, she knew she should have been brave enough to contact the CEO and report him, whatever the consequences, but she felt powerless.

One evening, Cathy had stayed late to finish a job. The main office was empty, apart from someone packing up at the far end of the long room, when he suddenly appeared.

"It seems they've all gone home, doesn't it?" His eyes were glassy, his pupils dilated as he beckoned her. "Come into my office for a minute, would you?"

Cathy was hoping to get away soon, but he seemed to need her urgently, so she followed him, wondering what could be so important at the end of a long day. Something gnawed in the pit of her stomach when she watched him shut the door and close the blinds, but the alarm bells in her head didn't fully sound until he grabbed her arms and forced his chin into the crook of her neck.

"This is what you've been waiting for, isn't it, Cathy? You know it is," he told her as he pushed her down onto his sleek, leather sofa.

"No..." Cathy shook her head and tried to shove him away, but he had her arms firmly clamped at her sides.

"You do, you want me," Don insisted. "I've got great plans for your future, if you know what's good for you." He laughed as she freed a hand and gauged his cheek with her nails. "You know you've enjoyed the attention. You've made sure you were noticed, haven't you?"

"No! Get off me! Stop!" Cathy snatched her face away from his attempted kiss and desperately wriggled partly free, but he was too strong, and he knew it. The soundproof glass walls muffled her shouts. Anyone who might have been left in the building would never be able to hear her.

Don seemed to enjoy the battle, climbing off her as he said, "That was good, *really* good."

Cathy rushed for the door, grabbed her bag from her desk, and ran barefoot—hardly able to see through the tears streaming down her face. She somehow managed to hail a taxi and make it home in her shaken state, showering three times, desperately trying to get rid of the smell of him. She knew she was destroying any evidence of what he'd done, but at the time she didn't care. She couldn't see the point of going to the police. It would be his word against hers, and she knew who would win.

After all this time, the bullies have won.

She was never going back there. The next day, Cathy phoned in sick and posted her resignation. She spent six days curled up in her dressing gown between showering, scrubbing, and trying to pretend it didn't happen. She told her parents she had the flu.

The following week she registered at a temping agency, just to earn some money while she tried to get her life back on track. She knew she couldn't cope with the situation much longer, and she began to look for a way out. She was still in touch with some of her old friends from university, and one of them sent her a card:

"Hi, Cathy! Just thought I'd let you know I'm off to pastures new! I've landed myself a job in Sydney, and I've got my work visa, so I fly out in a few days. I'll let you know my new address when I get there. You'll have to come out for a visit—you'd love it out there! Hope to see you soon. Love, Jane."

The seeds were sown. Cathy began to explore her escape route. When she found an advertisement for what she thought was the perfect job—with a sponsored visa to go with it—she decided to send in an application. As she filled in the form, she mentally shrugged her shoulders and allowed fate to determine what happened next. One way or another, she was leaving London, and she didn't want to go back to her parents now. A humiliating return to telling them when she was going out, what time she'd be back, and who she was seeing was not something she could contemplate. She couldn't envisage settling down to life in the village, where she would suffocate under the scrutiny of every move she made and wither without any money to keep herself looking like a city girl instead of a country bumpkin. She couldn't worry them with what was going on, and she wasn't sure what her father would do if he knew.

Chapter Twenty-Four

Libby stared at the screen in front of her. She tried to ignore the list of people she might be related to, but it nagged away at her. It would be so easy to make that click, see who they were, maybe even find one out of curiosity. She scanned the list of possible matches, taken aback by the fact that there was a list at all. There was something not quite comfortable about realising that there were others deliberately trying to find her. What had begun as something light-hearted, nothing more than a bit of fun, was turning into something disconcerting—and yet compelling. How much information about herself had she given away? How much information were others perfectly willing to share?

She considered herself careful. She'd wiped her Facebook page when she left school, meticulously obliterating anything she had no wish for future employers to see. She hoped no one could ever resurrect the less-than-sober festival-going images of her sixth-form era. She shuddered at the thought of the V-signs and protruding tongues, the silly selfies reflecting streaming make-up and shots in hand before she was legally able to drink. She'd made sure her mother couldn't see them because her mother was not a friend and her privacy setting had been tight, but she knew it was safer to reinvent herself on social media from the time she started med school. She'd even avoided a profile picture showing herself, using the dogs instead.

Since Libby started her search for ancestors, to put together a family tree, she'd been parting with money she hadn't intended to spend. Like an addict, she was driven to follow a trail of clues to who might be the right people. She was doing as much as she could within the time limit set by the pay-as-you-go subscription, filling in the chart as well as she could. There was so much out there! She found several websites she could use to check and cross-check what she found—births, marriages, deaths, and census material that could pin down whole families. She could have asked her mother for help, but this was something she wanted to do on her own. Mum might not approve, and she didn't want to be stopped, so it was safest to avoid telling her in the first place. No one ever talked about the previous generations, and she knew the past had been a no-go topic for her grandmother, because of the war.

By the time the Easter holiday came, Libby had been able to work her way back to her great-grandparents. She had the key names she needed, but she could see no direct link with her DNA result and anyone in the list she had been given. There were Harrisons and Mitchells in her parents' generation, so that was relatively easy, but it started to become more complicated when she tried to go back one more generation. What were her grandmothers' maiden names?

Slowly, she gathered the strands she needed, discovering—with the release of the census returns for 1911—that some great-grandparents and grandparents had come from families of several children. It was frustrating that no later census material was available, so she could not be sure that she had found them all. 2021 was a long way off, and she discovered that census material was not released for a hundred years.

How she wished she could speak to her own grandparents, to ask them what they could remember. It had never seemed important, but now it felt as if these names on the screen in front of her were real people with real lives that connected to her, and she wanted to know them, somehow. She wondered why their memories weren't kept alive by her parents talking about them. She knew her grandfather had a brother who died in an accident, and she'd once heard mention of the name Phillip, but she wondered what he was like. *Did he look like her grandfather? And what did their parents do for a living?* She'd heard the story of how her mum's parents had met—it seemed so romantic to her—but it had never crossed her mind, until now, that they never talked about their childhood, or their brothers.

Libby's grandmother's brother had been a brilliant vet, a shining light to aspire to, but she'd never known him, even when she was little. It began to seem as if theirs was a tight little unit—just her immediate family—but that had never seemed out of the ordinary before. It was just the way it was.

As she looked at the black print on the white page, she began to feel the stirring of curiosity. She had no cousins on her mother's side because Cathy never had children, and she knew of only one on her father's side, but she hadn' t seen him since her father left. Her mother had cousins she didn't know well.

What was it with all of them? Why were they all so estranged? Had there been some major falling out in the past? Were there some villains or skeletons in cupboards that no one was going to expose? It could all be quite exciting if she could uncover some secret she wasn't supposed to know.

Her eye came back to the name that was suggested as a possible first cousin. *Who was this Vicky Thompson?* Libby pondered. *Thompson. Hadn't that been the name of that Mike who knew Belle's father?* She supposed it would be quite a common name. Maybe it would be worth just making contact, but the prospect was unnerving.

Chapter Twenty-Five

"Hello, sister of mine!" Vicky heard his usual fond greeting as she picked up the phone. "You back from Cornwall?"

"Hi, Mike. Yes. Where are you?"

"I'm in London at the moment, Vick," he explained cheerily. "I've been looking after Paul's flat while he's not in town and making sure it isn't wrecked by his daughter and a student friend. I was thinking of coming to see you at the weekend. Is that OK? Can you cope with your wayward brother dropping in?"

Vicky knew banter was his way of saying that he loved them all and wanted the reassurance of seeing, for himself, that his father had really recovered.

"Of course. I'll tell you all about our trip. I've got some interesting news for you."

"Really? What's that?"

"Wait till you get here," Vicky said in a playful tone. "Don't worry. It's nothing that's going to affect you."

"Right. OK. I'll see you on Friday, then. Bye for now."

"Bye. Drive carefully."

"Who, me? Of course, I will!"

Vicky could hear the grin in his voice, unconvincing as it was. She wished he could not afford fast cars. She knew Georgie and her dad would be thrilled to have Mike visit, and she wondered how he would react to her discovery of family secrets.

Since Cornwall, she had revisited her half-hearted attempt at genealogy. It had been a long time since she had started trying to build a family tree for Georgie, and Bob's accident had put paid to anything but his recovery being a priority. Vicky remembered she'd sent in a

DNA sample before the accident, when he told her about his mother's letter. She knew he would have been troubled by his discovery after Peggy's death, and she wanted to help him to trace the truth, but she wondered how wise it was to dig up a past that had been buried for so long, and what it would achieve. She was afraid he would just be hurt.

Vicky tried to imagine what it was like not to know your birth parents, not to have that certainty of who you are like. It was as if something had begun to unravel, like a reel of cotton dropped and rolling across the room, and she wasn't sure that they could catch it and rewind the thread. They all sometimes wondered where Mike's dark hair came from—everyone fair but him. As her mother would say, he could charm the birds from the trees, and his love of a challenge had made him highly successful, but neither of her parents had been as extroverted as he was. Not knowing was not a problem when no one thought about it, but once the unravelling began, she could not dismiss the questions in her mind.

Vicky picked up a pencil and took a piece of paper from the printer, so that she could start to scribble down the names she now knew about:

Great grandparents	Grandparents	Parents
1. David and Bronwyn Hitchin. From Cornwall	1. Penny Hitchin and ? Mitchell. From where?	1. Caroline (Mitchell) Hitchin and Bob Thompson.
? Mitchell		No known siblings.
2. Unknown	2. Unknown	
	3. Robert and Peggy Thompson	

Vicky stared at the paper in front of her, then drew an arrow from Penny to a note saying, "Brother in Australia. Son, cousin to Caroline = Thomas David Hitchin + brother unknown."

Too many unknowns. She was about to toss the page to one side in frustration, when something suddenly registered. Penny married a

Mitchell and moved away. *What was the name of that girl who was a DNA close match?* Vicky tried to remember.

A surge of energy, as if she had been electrocuted, catapulted her towards her laptop, where she tapped impatiently on the worktop, waiting for it to boot up. *Why did it always take so long, when you were in a hurry? Bingo!* There it was. Braithwaite. Family tree shows mother a Mitchell. So, she could well be related, it seemed. Even if she wanted to let go now, she could not shake herself free of the grip of coincidence. Like a twisting rope, this puzzle was wrapping itself around her, and it seemed the more she tried to shrug it off, the more determinedly and tightly it hung on.

Chapter Twenty-Six

They'd been putting it off, but Cathy and June knew they needed to clamber back into the loft. Cathy needed to find the photo albums her mother said she was to have, and both sisters knew that they'd only begun digging into the clues to their mother's hidden past. They'd been rocked by the revelation that their mother gave birth to a baby before she was married. They couldn't help but pity that girl whose parents seemed to abandon her, and as they assimilated what they knew, they were driven to find out more about what happened to their mother and the baby.

They couldn't call him their brother—not yet. There lurked a subconscious fear that a person they didn't know—who could be anywhere or anyone—existed. June began to wonder whether she could ever have walked past him in the street without knowing.

"Do you think he knows about us?" ventured Cathy, as they pulled down the ladder again.

"Who knows?" replied June. "He's in the will, but it doesn't say he knows her. It sounds as if she has never set eyes on him since she gave him up. If he tried to find her, he obviously didn't succeed. Just as well! What if he's a crook or a thoroughly despicable person?"

"That's what I was thinking. It's unnerving. What has she set in motion with her legacy, June? Should we just keep quiet about what we know, or do we tell the solicitor and let someone try to find him?"

"We say nothing for now. We need to know what we're dealing with, as far as we can. We'll have to carry on searching, see what we've got. Then we'll decide."

"I just feel I don't like him already," Cathy admitted in a low voice. "It feels as if he can just rock up and take what should have been ours, including part of our mother's past."

"We can't own her past, Cathy. It is there. He is there, somewhere, because he is part of her past, and that makes him part of our present, whether we like it or not."

Cathy felt a stirring of the old mistrust of men who would trample over women to get what they wanted. *How do we know he's not just another one out for what he can get?* They abandoned the difficult conversation as they climbed back into the loft and made their way to the boxes they'd begun to explore. It was only when they moved the old rug that they could see a tea chest sporting a large, white label with faded writing on it. June shone a torch on it, and they could just about make out a list of contents, including albums of photographs from 1950 to 1970. The two women pulled off the old brocade curtain that protected the contents from dust and began to lift out the items one by one, carefully placing them on the wooden boarding under their feet.

"I don't remember seeing these before, do you?" asked June.

"No," answered Cathy, absorbed by the thickly padded, once-white volume that was very obviously a wedding album. "All we ever saw was a few loose photographs, wasn't it? I had no idea there were so many albums up here! There seems to be one for every year! Look, the later ones are colour!"

"I suppose these are what Mum wanted you to have," said June. "But how on earth did she think you would be able to transport them?"

"Maybe," Cathy slowly uttered, "she thought I would come home and never go back. Maybe she hoped I would stay once we didn't have her to keep us in touch. There's no way I can take these back on a plane, is there? She must have had a plan!"

The effort to get the albums out of the loft was daunting. As the key turned in the front door, and the twins could be heard downstairs, June decided they needed help. Leaving Cathy to sort the albums into decades, she clambered down the ladder and recruited two unenthusiastic supporters. She spread an old chenille cloth over the dining table, ready to receive the offerings as they emerged into daylight for the first time in years. She posted Alex at the bottom of the ladder and Millie at the bottom of the stairs, so they formed a human chain. She put herself on emptying the tea chest and Cathy on passing the volumes down to Alex. A few at a time, they managed to gather the albums on the table, and June produced a damp cloth to remove the dust they brought with them, despite all the care.

Releasing Millie and Alex, who went in search of after-school snacks, June and Cathy started to look through the photographs, starting with 1950. They looked at the wedding photographs and wondered who were all these people they had never met. Some were duplicates of official prints their mother once had on the wall—the happy couple smiling on their special day, posing outside the church against the backdrop of the bell tower, Maggie's dress fit for a princess.

In a photo of the wedding guests grouped by the fountain Cathy recognised from her visit to the Hall, they could see someone who looked like their mother and assumed it must have been her brother. The men all sported the traditional top hat and tails, while the women rivalled each other in hats and gloves, some in high heels and the latest full-skirted dresses, tight at their waists. The man to Maggie's left must have been her father. Next to him was her mother—an attractive, middle-aged woman with her hair in a French pleat and her dress and jacket finely cut. And there behind Maggie's husband, was another man whose hair fell over his left eye, just as Sam's had. With a slightly thinner face, the similarity was so strong that it had to be his brother—the one that was killed. The sisters thought that maybe that was his wife next to him.

June and Cathy's fascination led them on to look at more, each tiny black and white print carefully stuck into the album with corner brackets, arranged on the page and labelled with a date and location.

As they flicked through, they saw snaps of seaside trips and special occasions. In one album were photos of the coronation celebrations, with Cathy and June's mother standing near some children and a woman who might have been their mother. By the time they had waded through twenty years of highlights and change, it was like flipping through time-lapsed images of their whole family. They laughed at some of the clothes and hairstyles—the stiletto shoes of the fifties and the plastic boots of the 60s. They'd never thought of their mother as young and stylish, or their father as a dashing young man, so it was like meeting strangers in the photos, and it hit them that time passes so quickly in hindsight.

The sisters' childhood appeared in plastic pockets, the number of photographs multiplying as they reached the era of cameras that could take 35mm negatives on a roll of film.

"Oh, look at us in this one, June, in our imitation suede jackets! We thought we were so cool! Did I really swagger like that?"

"At least that's not as embarrassing as the holiday photos, is it? Just look at these! That was a perm, wasn't it?"

They were in danger of giggling like schoolgirls again when Cathy's smile faded. "June, you know I can't take these albums, don't you? But we can't just throw them away. Why don't we scan them in a few at a time? It'll take ages, but at least then I'll have them, like Mum wanted—just not in albums. We should leave this lot here for your children like a family heirloom, shouldn't we?"

"Good idea! It would be good for the kids to inherit them eventually. We may have to ask Alex to make scanning these a summer holiday project."

Supper was going to be late. June could already hear the twins rummaging through cupboards in the kitchen. For a few minutes she felt like a terrible mother, but then she told herself that Millie and Alex were old enough to be helpful, if they felt like it, and they could have made a meal for her. Even so, she had to leave Cathy to close the loft while she tackled making a speedy lasagne.

Cathy went back up to the chest to replace the curtain cover. It felt as if they had taken the lid off a coffin that day, releasing a darkness hovering behind the present lives in the gene pool—swimming around in them and the lifestyle part of their inheritance. She felt a long continuum stretching back into the past and on into the future, with her and June sitting somewhere on it for as long as they were allowed to be there. They had to be custodians of what the others cared about.

Cathy was still thinking about it that night when she opened an email from her friend Karen back home. Karen knew her so well; she always knew just what to say, her condolences always a bit deeper and more comforting than anyone else's.

"*I can't help but think of that quotation we saw from Djon Mundine, Aboriginal Curator at Campbelltown Arts Centre,*" Karen's message said. "*I don't remember the quote exactly, but he spoke about what made up 'dreaming' for Aboriginal people in everyday life, didn't he? Maybe we would do well to follow the concept, making for ourselves a dreaming time, gathering together what we can to draw from memories and thoughts, as he suggested. You'd be great at working on the 'imagine and create' he referred to.*"

Cathy smiled as the words touched her. She remembered the quotation. Maybe the photo albums being left to her was her mother's way of telling her she needed to see herself in this context, not as an individual who could separate from all that contributed to who she was, but linked to the memories and building on them. Mothers were often wiser than you knew. She thought maybe the Aboriginal people had worked that out.

Chapter Twenty-Seven

Vicky knew her brother had arrived when she heard his engine roar up the drive and the gravel protested as he came to an abrupt halt. Georgie was already out the door as Mike climbed out of his car.

"Hiya, little man!" Mike gave him a man-hug and ruffled his hair, Georgie only forgiving the latter because he loved both his uncle and the car. "How's the old man?" he asked, as Vicky caught up with her son.

"He's doing well, really well. He enjoyed the Cornwall trip. I'll show you the photos when you've had a cup of coffee. Come on in."

Mike kicked off his shoes as he entered the house, a habit he'd never shaken, trained as he was by their mother when he'd lived at home. He felt the cold of the tiles through his socks until he reached the lounge, and the armchair near the fire. The grate gave him a cold welcome, but he knew it was where their father liked to sit, and that made it a favourite.

"Oooh, you'll have to get out of there when Dad arrives!" laughed Vicky, carefully setting down mugs on coasters. Georgie sat himself on the floor, leaning against the legs of Mike's chair.

"So, what's all this about you having something to tell me? Do I have to wait till you've shown me every single photo you took in Cornwall?"

"Well, in actual fact we can do both at the same time."

Mike frowned, wondering what kind of riddle his sister was using just to frustrate him.

Vicky reached for her phone, ready to feel the familiar resistance to being bored by her photos. "You'll have to come and sit next to me, Mike. I can't show you properly otherwise."

"Oh, OK. I'll give you ten minutes!" he exclaimed with a brotherly grin. "Then your time's up, and we're going to the pub for lunch as soon as Dad arrives. You can be my timekeeper, Georgie. Here, take my watch."

Georgie obliged and planted himself in the seat Mike had vacated.

Vicky started by showing Mike the photos of the coast, and they shared their memories of time there as children. He looked at the photos of St Eval as she explained how they had found the old airfield and the church that had been the lookout tower during the war. He became genuinely interested in what they had seen, and how it linked to the granddad he remembered so fondly. Talking about him gave Vicky the opportunity to lead gently into the next group of photographs. Without an explanation, she put the photo of the cottage, with its large iron gates in front of him.

"Wait a minute! I know this place, don't I? Is it what I think it is?" asked Mike, wishing the phone screen were larger, so that he could scrutinise the photo more carefully.

"You do," said Vicky. "It's where our grandparents lived. We found it!"

"Wow! Could you see through the gates, Vick?"

"We did better than that. The man who lives there now saw us peering, and he invited us in."

"That was risky, wasn't it? What made him think you weren't a band of robbers come to do your worst?" grinned Mike.

"Maybe the fact that he knew who we were," began Vicky, pausing quite deliberately to let the words sink in.

"What? How could he? You're joking, aren't you?"

"Nope. Not joking at all. He asked who we were, and when we told him, he let us in. I had to show him my driving licence, but that was all. Guess who he was!"

"No idea! The old gardener, or someone who knew Mum when she was young? Someone who's always lived in the village?" Mike seemed excited to make his guesses.

"Close, but not close enough. It turned out that he's our mother's cousin, so he's our first cousin once removed. I looked it up!"

"So how come we didn't know about him, then?"

"That's where the rest of the story comes in," Vicky began, and she gave Mike the outline of what had happened to the relatives they never met. When she finished, she took a large gulp of her tea, giving Mike a chance to adjust his thoughts.

"Time's up!" called Georgie, just as Vicky reached the end of the tale. It had been more than ten minutes, and Georgie had been listening too hard to watch the time. He'd only just woken up to the fact that he was supposed to be looking at the watch—tossing it into Mike's lap and running up the stairs to his room.

Vicky relaxed. There were some things he'd be better not hearing. She could assume only another ten or fifteen minutes before Georgie came bounding back down.

"So now we know why Mum wasn't comfortable with her parents, don't we?" Mike marvelled. "She must've known about her cousin and his father, and maybe she, too, found the church thing too restricting. She never said a word, did she?"

"No. Even Dad didn't know the whole story. He doesn't know I've been trying to fill in some of the blanks in our family history, either."

"What have you been up to? You know the saying 'Be careful what you wish for.' You could uncover skeletons that are best left in cupboards."

"Well yes, but once you start, it grabs you, and you want to know more. I discovered some papers while Dad was in hospital, but he doesn't know I found them. He'd been trying to find his birth mother."

Mike scrunched his brow. "I thought she was dead."

"So, did I. So did he, I think, but he must have found his adoption papers after Gran died. There was a letter from his mother. He'd found out who she was, and who she married. It looks as if that's why he had gone to Ackerthwaite on the day of the accident. It didn't seem important at the time, because he was so ill, but it wasn't on his way to anywhere he usually goes."

"What's he doing about it now? Do you know?"

"No," Vicky said. "I don't think he's tempted fate any further. Maybe he's decided to leave the past in the past. But now I know who both of our grandmothers really were, and it's pretty intriguing, isn't it?"

"If you can be bothered to be intrigued, Vick. Not sure I want to know any more. Better to let sleeping dogs lie. He could walk into a whole lot of trouble if someone has been hiding a secret all these years, and what would he gain?"

"It's just the knowing, isn't it, though? Maybe he needs to satisfy his own curiosity. I'll wait and see. If I get a golden opportunity to talk to him about it, without letting him know I read those papers, I'll test the waters."

There was a sound at the front door, and Georgie came running down the stairs as he heard his grandfather arriving, jumping the last two steps just as Mike turned the latch.

"Hello, son!" Bob beamed at Mike as they headed for an embrace of mutual affection, Georgie trying to get between them for a group hug.

While they greeted each other, Vicky collected coats in preparation for the walk down to the Rifleman for lunch. She felt a rush of love for these three generations of men-folk, each of them reflecting another in some small way. Maybe she could understand the need to know who came before you, who provided the gene pool that made you.

PART SIX

"Be careful what you wish for, lest it come true."
- frequently attributed to an old Chinese proverb.

Chapter Twenty-Eight

Sitting in the shade outside the cafe on Fremantle's Cappuccino Strip, Jim lingered, not wanting to make the call he knew he had to make. Sally had been so excited when she'd given him the news that she was expecting their baby, and he'd been elated. They'd waited a long time, making sure they earned enough to buy the house they dreamt of in a good suburb of Perth, where their family would have every advantage they could give them.

Jim considered himself extremely lucky to land the job in Cathy's fledgling company, where he would prove himself quickly and win her trust—along with a salary that secured their future.

He was a happy man. He knew the business inside out by the time Cathy had taken off for the old country, and he knew he could hold the fort for her a while, as long as she made the decisions he needed her to make. She hadn't given him a date for her return, and now time was ticking past. He knew he had to tell her that when the baby arrived, he would be needing to take parental leave, and he didn't think Cathy would be paying him more than she had to if he was absent. She didn't have anyone else who could step up, either. Somehow, he had to break the news to her, and he didn't think he could do that via email. He would have to phone her. Right now, she might just be getting up. Should he do it now, or wait till later?

Giving himself thinking time, Jim walked down to the water's edge. He wandered aimlessly around the harbour, gravitating towards the memorial to the migrant children at Victoria Quay. He had often stared at it, wondering what it was like for over three thousand children in care who were sent across the world to populate this country between 1947 and 1953, his own grandfather one of them. *How terrifying it must have been to be alone, wrenched away from family and friends,* he thought. *How tragic for the family that lost them for ever.*

Jim had it drummed into him, from a very young age, that family was precious, and every moment you could devote to your child was one you have not wasted. His own parents had been wonderful role models for him and his siblings, working hard to provide them all with a good Catholic education and making each of them feel cherished. They were thrilled at the thought of a baby on the way, every one being seen as a blessing, whatever the circumstances. Jim would have something to live up to, if he was to be as good a parent as they'd been to him. Family first.

Chapter Twenty-Nine

Libby agonised with herself, but finally decided that she'd better tell her mother before she started making contact with people that might be related to them both. She wasn't sure what to do, her curiosity saying one thing and her caution another. She had no way of putting further pieces of the jigsaw together, and at the moment it seemed to be a picture with a big hole in it. She'd been able to trace her grandparents' marriages on her mother's side and her father's, thanks to snippets of information she registered, but without more details, she couldn't go far enough back to find much more than she already had.

What she did find was her grandmother's brother, and surprisingly, a possible brother for her grandfather, but they were all born too late for the 1911 census to confirm family groupings. She was giving up now, but the tantalising link with someone sharing some DNA was tempting her to find out as much as she could. When it came to her mother, she thought it best to tread carefully.

"Hi, Mum," she said when June picked up the FaceTime call. She talked about what she'd been doing, what she was studying, what gigs were coming up, and it was only near the end of the call that she plucked up the courage to say, "Do you remember how I sent off that DNA sample a while back?"

"No," came the reply. "I didn't know you did that. What on earth made you do it? I didn't think you were interested in that sort of thing, other than the science."

"Oh, I thought I'd told you. A few of us decided to see what came of it, and I thought maybe I'd find out where my red hair came from." Libby laughed nervously, trying to make light of her own words. "I didn't take it seriously. I thought I'd just get a load of waffle about being fifty percent this and twenty percent that, and it would all just amount to being born in a country that had been conquered a few times in ancient history."

"So, were you, then?" Encouragingly, Libby could hear the smile in June's voice. "Is your red hair Viking?"

"Well, yes and no." Libby paused, taking a deep breath. "I got the proportions, and there was nothing surprising in them, but I did get one surprise."

"Oh! What was that, then?"

"Well, it seems there is someone out there who is a close relative. The website's suggesting a first cousin, which is a bit spooky. She's someone called Vicky, and I haven't got a cousin called Vicky, have I?"

June felt the blood drain from her face, and she was glad that Libby probably couldn't see her well enough for it to be obvious. Her smile was fixed as she tightened the muscles in her cheeks. "Not that I know of," she answered truthfully.

"Strange, isn't it? I was wondering whether to get in touch with her, find out who she is, and how she fits into our family. I'm sure it's just something very boring, but it's bugging me. What do you think, Mum?"

"I wouldn't do anything rash, Lib. You don't know who these people are out there. They may not be very nice. It's a heck of a risk. Why don't you leave it for now, and we'll have a chat when you come down for the weekend? We should maybe see what Cathy thinks, eh?"

"OK. If you say so. I thought you might be curious as well, but yes, we can have a family summit, if you like. I'll show you the results I got though, if you'd like to see them."

"That would be great. I can see what an incredible patchwork of genes you are!" June regained her composure, feeling that she had this under control now. "So, we'll see you soon then, love. Take care. Love you."

"Love you too, Mum. Give the twins an embarrassing big sisterly hug from me."

"Will do. 'Bye."

As the screen went blank, June allowed her face to relax. She instinctively pulled her fleece around her, feeling chilled, and her fingers followed their own inclination to fiddle with the zip, as if it were a string of worry beads.

So, there was a cousin called Vicky. She must be related to the brother they'd never met. The last thing she wanted was for Libby to befriend someone they might yet find themselves resenting, someone who might be part of a problem they had yet to face. It felt as if a huge shadowy figure followed her across the room and up the stairs, watching her, wondering what she would do next, and waiting with a demonic laugh to destroy the life she'd protected for so long. She was going to have to tell the children about the will before long. That meant telling them about *him*. But what should she tell? What could she tell?

So far, they'd discovered secrets their mother had left hidden, yet she obviously intended them to be set free when she died, or she wouldn't have included her lost son in the will and kept the evidence in her treasures box. And if she wanted the secret to be out, she and Cathy would have to let the solicitor know what they now knew, so this stranger could be found.

If Libby had found Vicky, Vicky could find Libby, and if they ignored the existence of the baby boy, the man could come knocking on their door. Part of her wanted to meet him, wanted to see what he had turned out to be. The other part of her was terrified at the prospect of sharing her mother with a stranger—one who could be anything. The possibilities were endless.

What if he's part of a gang? What if he's a gold-digger, determined to take away everything he possibly can? What if he's a thoroughly unpleasant person, or violent, or stupid? The more she thought about it, the more questions her mind tossed at her. *What does he look like? Is he dark, like the photo of the pilot, or fair, like our mother? Is he tall and slim, or short and fat? Is he rich or poor?* He could be anything and anyone, and she might have walked past him without knowing it. June had no idea where he was.

Cathy had said nothing about him for the last few days—they'd been focused on the discoveries in the loft—but it was time to face some hard truths. *He existed.* He was entitled. They should do the right thing.

June had absentmindedly tidied away the clothes that were in the airing cupboard, the mechanical actions of folding and storing calming her body, if not her mind. She could hear Alex softly playing his acoustic guitar, while Millie seemed to be practising dance moves—presumably with her headphones on.

Cathy had gone to bed early to read a book. The house was full of people, yet it seemed cloaked in an eerie quiet, almost as if the shadow would jump out at her and shout "Boo!"

Chapter Thirty

Cathy looked at the notifications on her phone—the usual newsy rubbish and junk mail—but then something caught her eye. A text. She didn't use text much these days, with all the other ways of keeping in touch with people, but there it was, from an Australian number. She clicked on it, not recognising it immediately, but then realised it was from Jim. Strange. He kept her up to speed with work via Skype or email or social media messaging, not text. She pulled up the message, wondering what it could be about. She began to read through the pleasantries at the start, but as she clicked on the dots to "see more," the real reason for contacting her became clear.

"Cathy, I feel dreadful having to tell you this, but the bottom line is that I'm going to have to take some leave, and you really need to come back in the next few weeks. The baby is due at the end of the month, and I'll be going on parental leave as soon as it arrives. I could ask Chanice to take over, but she doesn't know what I know, and she wouldn't be up to handling the large accounts. If you aren't here, you could lose them. I know it has been a difficult time for you, and I guess you are still sorting things out over there, but I couldn't put off telling you any longer. I'll Skype tomorrow evening. Jim."

"Damn!" said Cathy to herself, trying not to let anyone else hear. "Damn, damn, damn! How could he do this to me? Why did it have to be now? Oh God, I'm going to have to tell June tomorrow."

Sleep came fitfully, as Cathy tossed and turned, thinking and re-thinking what she would say to Jim and June. She'd become so enmeshed in the past—her past, her mother's past—that what was going on right now, halfway across the world, had been pushed to one side of her mind.

There had only seemed to be one relevant present, and that was where she was, trying to piece together what she knew and what she felt about the revelations that had come crashing into her life. She felt as if she were on a fairground ride, careering down into water that splashed up all over her. She needed to rewind the images and start it all again in some kind of logical order. A perfect stranger was dragging the past into her life, and she wasn't sure she was ready to meet it.

The next morning, Cathy dragged herself out of bed and made her way down to the kitchen, where the warmth of the Aga stove and the welcome of the dogs momentarily lifted her spirits. She made herself a mug of coffee and sat in the old rocking chair, comforting as it was when she was agitated. She remembered how, as a child, she loved to clamber up into it and rock as hard as she could until her mother spoilt her fun. She looked around the kitchen, so full of memories and echoes of family times, feeling its anchor that had been lifted for so long. This was where she grew into the independent young woman her mother wanted her to be. This was safe, whatever was going on in the world outside the cocoon her parents had created for her to return to. This was her springboard, from which she'd gone into the world and learnt to survive. As she thought about survival, she heard June on the stairs, and about a minute later the dogs' tails wagged so hard they should've fallen off. She came through the door already dressed, despite the fact that it was Saturday, ready to take the dogs for a walk as soon as she had gulped down a cup of tea. Each of them could sense the tension in the other—what they needed to say dangling, as if snared in the air, waiting until someone set it free. The absence of conversation screamed at them as they avoided each other's eyes.

As June pulled on her boots and wax jacket and reached for the dogs' leads, Cathy suddenly jettisoned herself out of the rocking chair.

"I'll come with you, shall I?" she offered.

"Oh! If you like, but you'll have to be quick. The dogs need to go out."

Cathy grabbed her coat from the rack in the hall and fumbled for Libby's wellies, the only ones the right size among the pile of shoes in the cupboard under the stairs. Within two minutes she was crossing the kitchen floor as June hovered in the doorway, and a blast of cold air chilled the stone flags.

They made their way down to the end of the garden and out onto the footpath that ran across the field beyond. June let the dogs off their leads, and Cathy took her chance to speak.

"June—"

"We need to tell the kids what we've found out," June interrupted.

"We need to tell the solicitor, too." Cathy looked down at the ruts in the field.

"We're going to have to face it, aren't we? He's out there somewhere, and we've got information that could help to find him."

"It's keeping me awake," Cathy admitted, rubbing the corners of her tired eyes. "We can't keep this to ourselves, can we?"

"No, we can't, and there's even more reason why. Libby had her DNA sample analysed. There's someone who's been identified as a probable first cousin. It could be, couldn't it? If she's found this cousin, then the cousin could find her."

"Oh my God! Has she made contact?"

"Not yet. I stalled her. Told her we'd have a chat about it when she comes for the weekend. But she's asking questions, Cathy. I think we're going to have to enlighten her, and that means I'll also have to tell the twins because they'll find out."

"I wonder what they'll make of it. It feels kind of wrong, doesn't it, when it's not our secret to tell?"

"But it's their right to know, isn't it? If Mum decided the cat could come out of the bag when she died, it's not up to us to put it back in, is it? We must accept that whoever this man is now, he was our mother's son, our half-brother, my children's uncle. He's part of our blood family, and it was obviously Mum's wish that we do right by him. She never forgot him. She must have grieved for him her entire life, wondering where he was, who he was, what he did. We can't begin to imagine what she must have been through, how she must have wished he would just turn up one day before she died. The more I think about it, the more I feel like crying for her. If someone had taken one of my children away, it would have crucified me. Thank goodness society has changed. She wouldn't have had to give him up if it happened now."

"What about Ed and other people in the village? They'll gossip, won't they?"

"Let them gossip, then. There's been enough hiding of the truth. I keep thinking about that quote about the past being a different country. They certainly did things differently then."

Cathy nodded, knowing it was time to deal with the blow her news would deliver. "June, there's something else."

"What now?" June's shoulders slumped and she didn't look like she could take much more.

"I've had a message from Jim. He's going on parental leave in a couple of months—if his baby waits that long. I'm going to have to start making plans go back."

There were no words that June could utter. If she tried, she knew she would cry. All she could do was turn to her sister and throw her arms around her as the dogs bounded back towards her. She blinked away her tears as she bent down and put them back on their leads. They turned back towards the house, heads bent into the wind and tattered thoughts meeting each other in halting conversation.

Chapter Thirty-One

"Enjoy yourself. It's later than you think." - Chinese proverb

When Libby got off the train, she would normally power walk up the hill towards the house, anticipating her welcome and looking forward to a top-up of family time. This time, she could feel the energy leaving her, as if it were going back down the hill as she plodded up it. She knew she faced a difficult conversation; one she didn't really want to have. She'd heard a note of panic in her mother's voice when she told her about Vicky, and what she hadn't told her was that it was too late; she'd already sent a message before she thought better of it and decided to tell her mother. Luckily, there had been no reply so far, but somehow, she got the feeling there was something not quite right, and she was about to be in a whole heap of trouble for meddling.

"Hi, Lib," said a cheerful Millie, as Libby reached the kitchen. "You OK? You look knackered!"

"When did you learn to say 'knackered?' Don't let Mum hear you saying that! I'm sure that hill gets steeper every time I come home!" She gave her sister a hug, just ducking the jam-smothered toast Millie held at arm's length.

"I know a lot of things Mum might think I don't know," grinned Millie. "And if you think my language is the pits, you should hear our brother when he's with his mates!"

"Hmmm. Well, I forget how old you two are sometimes. I s'pose I was no innocent when I was sixteen. Anyway, where's Mum?"

"She's just popped out to the supermarket. She said to tell you she won't be long. She's left you a sandwich on the worktop. I should warn you, she's a bit off today. Snappy. I think she and Auntie Cathy must have fallen out. They've both got faces like thunder this morning, and Cathy seems to be on the phone to Australia a lot. She's upstairs in her room. They seem to have been looking at old photos. They don't tell Alex and me anything, but maybe you can find out what's going on. Alex is playing rugby, and I'm off to the gym, so neither of us will be around till teatime. See you later." With that, Millie threw her gym bag over her shoulder, clamped the toast in her mouth, and headed out of the door.

Left to her own devices, Libby wandered into the lounge. *What photos?* she wondered. She looked around, but nothing was obvious. She went over to the window seat and pulled back the curtains. Ah! So, this was what Millie meant. There was a stack of old albums, some of them looking as if they had been around for a lot of years. She picked up a black one with a tassel hanging from the corner. Opening it carefully, she was instantly entranced by the old black and white images, each one mounted at its corners. She stared at the faces, trying to link them to someone she might know, but it was impossible to work out who might have looked like this when they were so young. *Could that have been Grandma?* She turned page after page until suddenly she became aware of someone walking towards her.

"So, you found them, then," Cathy said softly.

"Oh! Sorry! Is it OK if I look at them?" Libby asked, worried she was being nosy. "Who are they? Where did these come from?"

"They are what your gran left to me. They were in the loft, along with a lot of other stuff we haven't seen for years, if ever."

"So, they're yours? Who are these people? Are there any of you and Mum?"

Cathy slid into the window seat beside her niece. There didn't seem to be any point in stalling, despite the fact that she and June would have to say more about what was up there when they told them all about the baby. She turned to the back of the album. "Look. This is your mum and me on the beach. It says we were eight and two. That's me in nappies! This one next to it is our parents with their friends."

"Wow! She was good looking, Gran, wasn't she? It's a shame you can't see the colour of her hair or the flowers on her dress. I didn't know she ever wore skirts that short! She looks happy, doesn't she?"

"Yes, she does. She and Dad look so close." Libby put down the black album and picked up one that looked even older, a sort of maroon colour with a Chinese pattern on it. Like the black one, it was full of sugar-paper pages, this time with smaller photos. She opened it about halfway through.

"This is your great grandmother and great grandfather," Cathy said wistfully. "I just about remember seeing photos of them when I was small, but these must have gone into the loft years ago, and we didn't know they were there."

"So why has Gran left them to you, then?"

"I've been asking myself the same thing. It's as though she's trying to tell me not to turn my back on the past. She was a wise old thing, our mum, and I think she knew or guessed more than she let on. When I went to Australia, I tried to leave the past behind, but you can't really do that because to deny your past is to deny part of yourself—what made you who you are. I didn't think that mattered, but it does. The roots you came from are always there, even if you settle somewhere else and put down some more. We're linked back to these people in these photos—the children we were, the adults we sprang from, the line stretching back in time. You can't see it in black and white, but that's probably where your ginger hair came from—your great granddad. I think I remember Mum saying his hair was a sandy colour."

Libby was no longer sure who Cathy was talking to. She seemed to have gone into a kind of dream state, running her finger over the photographs, her glazed eyes saying more about her unspoken thoughts than the words that came out of her mouth.

Libby was relieved when she heard her mum call out. "Hello there! I'm back! Are you around, Libby?"

"In here, Mum! I'll come and put the kettle on, shall I?"

"Great idea! Come and give your mum a hug!"

Libby did as she was asked, thinking to herself that it was an unusual request, and noticing that Cathy didn't follow her.

The afternoon passed with cooking, walking the dogs, and sweeping up some of the millions of leaves that had deposited themselves on the paths and beds they would need to plant up in the next few weeks. As they tipped the last green tub full onto the compost heap, June took the opportunity to open the conversation about the DNA results.

"Libby, we'll wait till the twins get back, and then I think we all need to sit round the table, and you can tell us what you've found out about your DNA, and we can tell you what we've found in the loft. There's stuff we need to thrash out between all of us, I think."

"Right. If you like. What have you been discovering then?"

"Well, you've seen a bit of the albums, haven't you? There's some other stuff you might be interested in, but we need to include Millie and Alex, to be fair, and we have to tell you all about Cathy's plans to go back to Australia soon."

"So that's what's going on! I knew there was something! I don't see why that's such a big deal, though. She wasn't here before. She was always going to have to go back, wasn't she?"

"Yes." June said nothing more as she emptied the wheelbarrow and tipped it on end.

"Tell you what, Mum. Why don't we have an early big birthday celebration for you before she goes back? It's time you had some fun, and you could make some good memories, instead of just the gloomy ones. If we're going to have a family summit, let's do some planning!"

"Whew! The wisdom of the young! You know, that's not such a bad idea, my love. Maybe we should. I could at least celebrate with my sister, while she's still here."

"Maybe it's time you went out to visit her, Mum. You haven't been since Dad left, have you?"

"No, of course I haven't. I couldn't leave all three of you for Mum and Dad to look after, and I couldn't afford to take you all with me, even if I could have coped with the journey. And then, I couldn't leave Mum, could I? It's not like just going round the corner, is it? Twenty-one hours away, on the other side of the world. She chose to go. She can choose to come back, but this isn't her home any more, and she won't come often. I have to accept that." June's hands were animated as she spoke, a passion igniting in her voice. "To be honest, I almost dread her coming because I know I've got to say goodbye again. I don't expect you to understand. If I and my parents weren't important enough for her not to go, I am not going to be important enough for her to give up what she's got now. Do I really want to visit that, put myself through leaving her behind when I come back? I'm not sure." She turned away determinedly, but not quickly enough to hide her tears from Libby.

At the front of the house, the dogs were making a racket as the twins came in, starving as usual. In an instant, everything returned to its busy normality, and everyone sat down to demolish a huge cottage pie. Libby settled in at the table, feeling the weight of her mother's emotion wash over her. Most of the time she tried hard to be vegetarian, but her principles didn't extend to her mum's comfort food, and it didn't seem like the best time to make a fuss.

After the meal, Cathy cleared away the last of the plates and cutlery, and June announced, "Millie, Alex, I need your presence a little longer. It doesn't matter what you wanted to watch on the box or your computer screens—it's family summit time." She was dreading starting, but it had to be done. "We have quite a bit we need to talk about. Libby has some news to share, and Cathy and I have got to tell you a few things as well. Libby, would you like to start us off?"

Libby gave the twins the abridged version of her venture into family history, making them laugh about being drunk and wanting to know who to blame for her hair. She skimmed over the research she had tried to do and told them that she'd had a massive surprise when she looked at the results. If she had a cousin, so did they, so she managed to keep them listening.

June took over then, her hands gripping the edge of the table. "We can probably explain that, actually."

Three pairs of eyes were suddenly riveted on their mother's.

"You see, we have made a surprise discovery, too," June went on. "You remember that we had to go to hear what your gran's will said?"

A chorus of "Yes" confirmed that she had their attention.

"Well, it was a bit more complicated than we expected…" Before June knew it, she had tumbled out the story of her mother's earlier life, the one she had lived before any of them existed. "We have a half-brother somewhere, so maybe you really do have a cousin, too." She stopped, knowing she had given them a lot to take in.

Cathy only silently watched the teenagers from the opposite side of the table—her face pale and her posture stiff.

"Oh, poor Gran!" Libby's eyes widened, knowing what she had seen in programmes about young women of the time. "You mean she was an unmarried mother all those years ago? What did they do to her, Mum? Why didn't anyone help her?"

"It was 1945," June said with a helpless shrug. "The man she loved was killed, and in those days being pregnant and unmarried was like committing a crime. There would have been so much shame! We've found that her parents sent her away—people used to do that then, so that it was kept a secret. Sometimes, girls were thrown out by their families."

The F-word slipped out of Alex's mouth before he could stop it, and he looked down at the table.

Millie gasped, waiting for June or Cathy to jump on it, but when no one did she exclaimed, "They took her baby away?" Her voice was cracking. "That is so cruel! Do we know what he was called?"

Cathy finally spoke. "We found some things in a box. There was a photograph, and we think the father was a pilot. She kept a couple of things belonging to the baby, and it looks as if his name was Richard. We don't know what he's called now."

"There's more." June silently decided they might as well know it all and spilled the news about their mystery uncle's inheritance. "Someone has to find him, if possible. We don't want you to worry. It won't affect us living here, your gran made sure we won't be homeless." She knew she was gabbling now, and words were tumbling out too fast for her children to compute.

"So, we might meet him, then," ventured Libby, thinking how fortunate it was that she might not be in trouble for digging skeletons out of cupboards, after all. "But what about Cathy? She won't meet him if she's going back to Australia."

"You're going back? When?" asked Millie. *Why does everyone keep so much to themselves in this family?* "When were you going to tell us that one, then?"

"Soon, Millie. I didn't know until a couple of days ago. I haven't fixed a flight yet, but I was going to tell you. I couldn't stay for ever..."

"So, what about what we talked about earlier, Mum? Are we going to have a party? Is it going to be a goodbye party now, as well as an early birthday party?"

"Oh, that's a great idea, Libby! It would be so good to have the chance to celebrate June's birthday before I go!"

"I suppose you want us to help organise it then, Libs," Alex asked.

"You're dead right! I think we three should put our heads together, don't you? I think Mum should let us get on with it, not do the work herself. Let's see what we can come up with."

"Hang on a minute!" June protested. "What about Cathy and me being involved in our own party?"

"Nope. I think your children are going to rebel on this one," Libby disagreed. We can message each other, use our phones, email people. We don't need you to do any of that. You are to leave it to us."

So that was that. The drama June and Cathy expected had evaporated. Focusing on the tension of the revelations had left them unprepared for Libby taking over, but they were grateful that the emotions quickly dissipated, and the attention had channelled away from trauma, even if the thought of her children wrenching away control of the party filled June with trepidation. It could turn out to be an absolute nightmare.

Chapter Thirty-Two

"We are such stuff as dreams are made on..." - Shakespeare ***The Tempest***

The date for the party was eventually fixed, after much consulting of calendars, avoidance of gigs, deadlines, and appointments. Millie and Alex took on designing an invitation that could be emailed out to people they thought the two sisters would like at their party. Since they needed email addresses, the job was made a little easier because they had to ask June to provide them from her contacts list. June secretly sighed with relief, as this meant she had some kind of veto on who might, and who definitely wouldn't, arrive.

Libby was able to book the function room of the Hall. She was given permission to decorate the room in advance, without her mother knowing a thing about it. She and the twins agreed that the way to provide food was to ask everyone who was coming to bring offerings for a finger buffet. They gave themselves a couple weeks, so that it would be the end of half-term for the twins, though that made no difference to Libby's workload. She would just have to be super organised and get ahead, so she could risk another weekend at home.

Plans were just about in place, and emails were coming in—to the threesome's relief. As Libby was looking at the list, another email appeared, this time in her junk box. She might have deleted it, but for the fact that the address began with vickythompson2@vt.co.uk. She moved it to her inbox and risked opening it.

Hi, Libby.

Thank you so much for your message and your email address. Like you, I am intrigued by the fact that we could be first cousins because I have been trying to put together some family history for my son. Maybe we could exchange some more details, or even meet up one day, to compare family names? I'm a teacher. Both my mum and my dad were adopted as babies, but I have found names that would help me to make connections. I would just need to be careful, because I know there could be some details that might cause problems. We might have to keep some things to ourselves, but if you're willing to swap information, let me know.

Kind regards,

Vicky

Libby didn't dare reply immediately. She now knew exactly what problems there could be for her, and she hoped Vicky was far away. She wondered whether she would dare invite Vicky to come meet her family. How would the others react if she turned up at the party?

"No. Don't even go there," she told herself.

Cathy and June decided they'd better type up what they found out about their mother's past, so they had the details clear for the solicitor. One evening when they had the house to themselves, they spread out the "treasure" on the dining table so they could sort it into some kind of order and record it in a matter-of-fact way that belied the emotions that swept across their faces and quickened their heartbeats. They looked at the sum total of what their mother had kept as mementos, and they each saw, in their mind's eye, a tiny baby boy dressed in the matinee jacket and bootees in their mother's arms. They put the photograph of the pilot by the side of the bootees. Did he ever know that he was going to be a father, they wondered? They sorted the letters into date order, weaving them into a story of love and loss, and imagining Maggie returning to the village with her parents trying to pretend that nothing had happened. How sad that they never met their first grandchild!

Cathy entered into a Word document the bare bones of the story. The black ink on white paper seemed far too impersonal for something that happened to the woman they called Mum. When they were satisfied that they'd given enough detail, they printed out the account. June wrote a letter to go with it, and it was sent on its way. They were nervous about what they'd done, but June drove into town, and they posted it through the letter box of the solicitor's office, feeling a sense of relief that they had done the right thing. Whether or not the man could be found, and whether he wanted to read the account, they'd done what they could to honour their mother's wishes. Now it was up to fate to take a hand.

As Cathy and June posted their letter to the solicitor, another was winging its way elsewhere, inviting a Mr Robert Thompson to attend the offices of a Mr Smithson in Leeds, to discuss a delicate matter of an inheritance to which he might be entitled. His expenses would, of course, be covered by the estate.

Bob rarely had post these days, so when an official-looking brown envelope dropped through the letter box, he felt a flicker of irritation.

It's probably just more junk mail, he thought. *It never stops!* When he opened the letter from Mr Smithson, he almost shredded it immediately, thinking it must be a scam, but something made him fetch his glasses and read it properly. It looked official, and it seemed to be on good paper, but he could hardly believe that a firm of heir hunters had been looking for him. Someone was probably trying to get money out of him, but he was nobody's fool. He examined the heading on the letter, but he knew logos could be faked these days. He didn't have any distant relatives to leave him any money. He decided to look up the firm on the internet, check the address, and the staff list. It all seemed to match.

When Vicky phoned that evening, he told her about his "bolt from the blue" to test her reaction to it. She thought they could have made a phone call. It all sounded a bit fishy.

"Well, if you decide to go, Dad, you're not going on your own. It's half term soon, so why don't we try to take a trip to Leeds then? I think you should give them a ring and see if you can get some more information out of them before we make the trek up there. It'd be good if someone's left you a fortune, though, Dad, eh? Dream come true!"

"Dream on, Vicky! I've never known anyone rich, so I can't see that ever happening!"

"Maybe you've got some long lost relative out there." As Vicky said the words, she suddenly realised how true her joke could be. The first cousin had to be related to someone. Maybe it was time to tell him about her and confess what she'd found when he was sick.

Chapter Thirty-Three

On a bleak Thursday afternoon in February, when Leeds was emerging from a night of freezing fog, Bob and Vicky were confronted by the rush of traffic outside the station. It seemed that people and cars were coming from all directions, and Vicky clutched the precise instructions they'd been given.

The entrance to the imposing old building was flanked by columns, a remnant of the prosperity of a bygone age. Once inside, they followed the sign up the stone staircase to the first floor, where they found a corridor leading to a less-than-imposing wooden door. It sported a brass plaque, indicating the office of Smithson and Clark. They rang the bell, and a tall, thin man appeared, smiling kindly and inviting them to come in.

"Hello there," the thin man had said as he showed them into a waiting area. "You must be Mr and Miss Thompson. Do come in. Would you like to take a seat for a few minutes? I'll be back." With that, he disappeared through another door, this one obviously an original fixture with a large brass handle mounted on its thick oak surface.

They looked around, Vicky taking in the high ceiling, marble floor, and ornate cornicing. A little tired, it boasted a prestigious past. She became aware that they'd said nothing to each other since they sat down, and when she glanced across at her father, she saw him looking at his hands, his fingers interlocked and knuckles going white. She wanted to throw her arms around him, but she was afraid to break his fragile control as he held in check the anticipation of what he was to find out on the other side of that door.

The thin man reappeared, still smiling. "Come in, come in! Mr Smithson is ready for you now. So sorry to keep you waiting, but he was just finishing a phone call. DIY today, as his PA is on holiday. I'm Mr Clark, by the way. Pleased to meet you." He shook their hands and held the door open, leaving them to enter the inner office without him.

They approached the large mahogany desk, behind which sat someone more like their image of what a Mr Smithson should look like. He peered over his glasses, and had he not approached them with a friendly welcome, Bob would have felt as if he were up before a rather dishevelled headmaster, who'd forgotten to do his hair.

"I am delighted to meet you both," he began. "I hope you've had a good journey. Can I get you a cup of tea or something? Are you warm enough?" He gestured towards two palatial chairs facing him on the other side of the desk.

"We're fine, thank you," answered Bob. "Pleased to meet you. I gather there is something very important you want to show me that you couldn't send through the post."

"Well now, I think there's a bit of explaining to do, Mr Thompson." When h'd been through the formalities of checking what Bob already knew and what he was prepared to learn, he took a formal stance, delivering facts devoid of emotion, making it slightly easier for Bob to hear them. He then retrieved some photographs from an envelope on his desk.

"Your half-sisters have passed on to me a photograph of Bill, and a photograph of your mother as a young woman, which you may wish to see."

He paused, giving Bob a chance to take in what he was offering, then slowly slid the photographs onto his desk, facing Bob and Vicky.

Bob's eyes travelled back and forth between the two images of strangers in front of him, searching for his own features in these two young people. Of his father, he only saw a little resemblance around the mouth and ears, and perhaps in the kink in the hairline, but as he stared at his mother's face, it was as if a trick of a mirror was reflecting his young self back at him. There were his high cheek bones, his full lips and his neatly-shaped nose. The eyes were large and round. He could tell she must have had fair hair, wavy like his own. His stomach tightened, his mouth felt dry, and he could feel his blood pulsing through his temples.

Vicky, meanwhile, studied every detail and muttered, "Mike!" as she saw the dark colouring of the pilot's hair. So that was where his charm came from. Same smile, same slightly cocky angle of the head, same mop of dark hair and dark eyes. There was no colour, but she could imagine it, and how the dashing young man had won Maggie's heart. The realisation dawned that these could have been her grandparents. They *were* her grandparents, by blood, though they could never replace the grandparents she'd known and loved.

She wondered what her father was feeling. He hadn't moved, a frozen version of himself. At last, he looked up across the desk into Mr Smithson's eyes, his own glazed and somewhere far away.

Daniel Smithson reached down into a drawer and lifted out a bundle wrapped in tissue paper. He carefully put it in the centre of the desk and proceeded to unwrap the contents. He heard a sharp intake of breath from Vicky as he lifted the last piece of tissue. Bob's face remained expressionless, his body motionless, his eyes riveted on the tiny matinée jacket.

"This," Mr Smithson began haltingly. "We think this was probably made for you by your mother or your great aunt, with whom your mother stayed in Wales."

"Oh Dad! Imagine her keeping it all this time!" Vicky's voice began to break. "She didn't ever forget you, did she?"

"She certainly did not, Miss Thompson, as you will know when I read to you what I have already read to your aunts.

It sounded strange to be talking of her having aunts. She never had aunts before, and she was unsure how to feel about the discovery of them.

Bob sat back in his chair, releasing a sigh in a controlled breath. He held the arms of the chair as if he needed them to maintain his balance. He'd spent a lifetime handling pressure, but that was in the service of his country. This struck so deep inside, he felt as if someone had put a stake through his heart, stomach, or even his brain. The world slowed like a film shown at half speed. His extremities felt weak, as if he were waking up after the crash all over again. Vicky watched, helpless, as it took every ounce of his strength to control his feelings.

"Do you feel able to listen now, Mr Thompson? Would you like me to read you the will?"

"Yes please. Yes please. Go ahead."

Nearly an hour later, when the fog had lifted, Bob and Vicky emerged from the building into the sunlight of a crisp, clear day, their clouded thoughts separating them. Vicky was already thinking it was time they met these relatives. Her father should know who they were, if he was to inherit part of what his mother owned. He was reeling, trying to make sense of what his mother had done, dreading that these half-sisters would hate him before they even knew him. He felt too old to deal with all of this. It was too complicated. The past was the past, and maybe it was better that it stayed there. But he knew, deep down, that it collided with the present, and it wouldn't go back. He had to face this, deal with it, see where it took him. He'd dealt with worse and not crumbled, and now was not the time to fall apart. It was not just his past to own; it belonged to Vicky, to Georgie. They had a right to know these people who shared their genes. If he did nothing, they might one day resent him. He owed it to them to try.

In his inside pocket was the piece of paper Mr Smithson had given him. The address tallied with the place he had found before his accident. The names of two strangers identified his mother's other children. He had an email address and a landline number. It was time.

Chapter Thirty-Four

Libby was on her way home again, relieved that this time it was going to be a cheerful occasion, even if it was partly to say goodbye to Cathy. She'd got kind of used to her aunt being around, but she did feel a ripple of satisfaction that she was finally going back where she belonged, and they could be their own little family unit again. She knew the twins had sometimes found it difficult to have her around all the time, trying to be on their best behaviour and avoiding the arguments that usually punctuated their otherwise close relationship. She seemed a bit odd to them, sloping off for walks, hiding in her room to "read," or closeted with their mother in secret conversations. At least her accent had slipped back towards their Yorkshire one, and it didn't jar quite so much now. The way she dressed had become more like their mother's, too. But they could tell she didn't completely fit in, even though she'd worked at the pub for quite a few evenings and even gone to church once or twice.

The twins had managed to set up access to the function room this evening, so that everything could be ready for tomorrow. They had actually stepped up and been quite responsible and grown up, much to Libby's surprise.

Earlier that day, a phone call had interrupted the preparation of canapés and taken June and Cathy by surprise.

"Hello. Who is this, please?" Cathy didn't recognise the voice asking for her or June.

"I'm so sorry to disturb you, but my name is Vicky Thompson."

Cathy felt her stomach tighten. They'd been expecting some news, as Mr Smithson had told them that their mother's son—the man they could not yet call brother—had been found.

"Thompson? So how can I help you?" Cathy knew she could have sounded excited, but instead her fingers clenched nervously round the phone.

"I'm Bob Thompson's daughter." A pause heightened the tension between them.

What is she expecting me to say? Cathy wondered, her brain blanking any constructive thought.

"My brother and I have come to Yorkshire with our father, to see where his mother came from. I do hope you will understand. I'm sure this is all as strange to you as it is to us, but suddenly we have a whole family we know nothing about. Look, we don't want to intrude, but we're staying at the hotel in the village, and he was just wondering whether it's possible to meet you while he's in the area." *He wants to meet his sisters,* she wanted to say. *Please be thrilled.*

Cathy wanted to say, "No! Go away and leave us alone!" but she knew June would want to see him, and a stirring of curiosity began to temper her mistrust. *He's a man. He'll think he can get his own way.* She tried to muster some enthusiasm in her business-like tone. "I'm sure it can be arranged, Miss Thompson. I'll talk to my sister. Can I take your number, and one of us will get back to you to agree a time?"

She wrote Vicky's number on the notepad by the phone. As they said their goodbyes, she was aware that she'd offered no welcome, as June would have done. She would leave the return call to her sister.

"He's staying the Hall!" Cathy said urgently as soon as she found her sister. "I just hope he doesn't end up gate-crashing the party, June. What if he wanders around and sees us? It could ruin the evening!"

"Calm down, Cathy," June responded, calmly scraping the last of the cake mix into the tins and putting them in the oven. "He's never seen us, and even if he's seen a photograph, he's highly unlikely to bump into us. It'll be fine. We just carry on as if he isn't in the building. Luckily, we can get to the function room without going through the hotel reception."

"Well, I guess at least being at the party would mean we can't sit around worrying about the meeting."

After Cathy's initial panic, and some almost-burnt butterfly cakes, they were determined to focus on enjoying their celebration. It crossed June's mind that they could invite him to join them, but she had a feeling Cathy wouldn't agree, and she wanted the day to pass in total harmony, so she didn't even suggest it. It was good to see Cathy smiling, positively enjoying herself, and nothing was going to spoil that.

June rarely went to functions, and Cathy had a limited choice of what to wear in her luggage. As they shared a glass of Prosecco, June produced the contents of her wardrobe.

"What do you think, Cathy? The navy dress or the cream trouser suit? I never seem to have the right thing for 'smart casual' occasions! Is this too fussy?" June held up a crimson top with beads sewn into a flower pattern, enjoying the sisterly closeness reminiscent of their teenage years.

"You can't show me up in that! I didn't bring anything posh with me!" laughed Cathy. "Why can't you just wear a pair of trousers and a shirt? Let's stick to casual—without the smart—and relax!" As she heard herself utter the words, she realised how she'd adjusted her priorities since she came back to England. "Didn't Libby say this was dress-down, anyway?"

June settled on a floral shirt-blouse over a pair of black trousers, totally appropriate for hosting, so Cathy could wear something almost identical. This way they could claim to be doing a sister act complete with flat shoes that wouldn't kill their feet by the end of the evening.

"Bliss!" thought June, slightly amazed that Cathy had agreed to this. In fact, Cathy had not worn those ridiculous high heels for a while now, and that could only be a good thing. They did each other's hair, just as they had years ago, and shared jewellery from June's collection of Marks and Spencer and Pandora, neither wanting to wear any of the more expensive items that had belonged to their mother. When they were satisfied that they looked passable, they set off up the hill, arm in arm.

Vicky had booked two twin rooms at the hotel for a long weekend, with the option to cancel. Mike was going to join them, and they were all going to look around the area. Vicky had sent a message to Libby, and she nervously awaited a reply. Bob was going to take the phone number with him to see whether he could make a brief visit to his half-sisters, since they'd indicated they were prepared to meet him. He wasn't sure whether feeling sick was because he was excited or terrified, as they drove past the fountain and pulled up in the car park.

The officious young woman at the reception desk gave a practised smile as she prepared their room keys and began to walk towards the stairs. "If you'd like to come with me, I'll show you to your rooms. You'll be on the first floor, where you'll have a stunning view of the gardens. I should just warn you that there may be some party noise tomorrow evening, but it shouldn't disturb you. You might just find the bar rather busy, but the function room is in another part of the hotel. If there are any problems, do please call reception. Here we are." She stopped outside two adjacent rooms. "Mr Thompson, this is your room, and Miss Thompson, this is yours." With a majestic sweep of her hand and a stiff bow of her head, she indicated that she would leave them to settle in.

When Mike arrived, he was just in time for dinner, and the group had a meal together in the hotel restaurant.

"Look, I can't sit here being stared at by stuffed animals and birds. This place is stuck in a time warp! The waiter is like something out of a period drama. How about I go to the bar and we take a drink up to our rooms, so we can relax?" Mike made a magnanimous gesture to avoid sitting in the restaurant any longer than her had to.

"OK, but we were warned the bar might be busy tonight," offered Vicky, her brother's fidgeting confirming that he was so far out of his comfort zone that he needed to escape. She sensed it was not just the surroundings that made him twitchy.

"Right. I'll be a few minutes, then. You go ahead, and I'll meet you upstairs." Mike took their orders and strode off. He soon understood why it was not such a good idea, as he edged his way through the throng and waited to be served. He finally reached the front of the queue as the crowd thinned and people seemed to disappear. Making his way upstairs, he heard a huge cheer go up and a rousing rendering of "Happy Birthday to You" coming from the function room at the back of the hotel.

Someone's having a good time, he thought. He'd quite like to be having one himself. *What has Dad let us all in for?*

"Can I take your coats, ladies?" asked Alex, as they arrived to a raucous welcome from the assembled guests. Libby was greeting people, Millie passing out an initial drink of sparkling wine or orange juice.

"They seem to have it splendidly under control, don't they?" June observed, and the sisters were very soon immersed in talking, drinking, and eating. Alex had set up some speakers for background music, and after the speech and the cake, the melodies grew louder, the food diminished, and someone started the dancing.

"Dangerously approaching dad dancing, isn't it?" chuckled Millie. "But these old folks seemed to be enjoying it."

In the room on the ground floor, there was much cheering as June blew out the assortment of pink, blue, and white candles on her birthday cake. The twins had thought about trying to fit fifty onto it, but they couldn't find that many, so they had made the shape of a five and a zero instead. They felt quite pleased with themselves when they found two tiny koalas to adorn the sides of the cake stand, taken from key rings Cathy had given them. They borrowed their mother's boomerang to complete the display. Everyone thought the balloons and banners and tinsel borrowed from the Christmas box were spectacular, and everyone who'd promised to bring food turned up with something. Soon, two tables were covered with plates of sausages, sandwiches, all sorts of savoury treats, and some delicious puddings to follow.

Libby rattled a spoon in a glass to silence the chatter as she stood on the steps of the stage. Cathy, guessing what was coming next, backed into the shadows in the corner of the room, hiding herself behind a tall man and his partner. Most people in the room were strangers to her, and her discomfort mounted as she prayed that no one would want to call her into the spotlight.

"Ladies and Gentlemen, my siblings and I would like to thank everyone for coming tonight, to celebrate our fantastic mum's fiftieth birthday and to wish our Auntie Cathy bon voyage. It is very much appreciated. We know they will find it difficult to part again, but we hope to make tonight a special memory for both. Please raise your glasses to June and Cathy!"

"To June and Cathy," echoed the voices round the hall as glasses were lifted into the air. Others made speeches about how they'd known June and how they hoped the two sisters would have a better year to come.

Cutlery tinkled over the backdrop of tasteful music and there was a contagious hubbub of touching conversations about lasting friendships capable of surviving distances.

Cathy did her best to avoid searching eyes, keeping to edges of the merry crowd. June was left to be thrust forward by Millie, taking a mock bow to her guests.

"Come on, Auntie Cathy," Alex said quietly, suddenly at her side. "You can't escape helping to cut the cake."

Cathy looked up at him, and he locked eyes with her, sending a firm message that she wasn't going to wreck their plans. She nodded to him, allowing herself to be led to the table where June waited. Phone cameras flashed around the room as the two sisters stood like bride and groom, holding the carving knife between them and smiling at the guests, then at each other, as if making a solemn promise to stand together from now on. It would be a photograph to be treasured by both of them in future years, each displaying it in a frame on opposite sides of the world, each proudly telling people, "That's my sister."

A new beginning, Cathy thought. *Yes. That's exactly what I need. No more hiding from demons from the past. I've got to face them, deal with them, and find a new way to be happy. I need to treasure my sister, talk to her more, visit her more, and care more than I've let myself care.* It was terrifying, opening that locked door inside her, and it made her feel incredibly vulnerable, but she felt again the closeness they'd known in their youth—felt like part of a family. *I can't lose it this time.*

At the end of the evening, June and Cathy insisted on walking back home, while Libby and the twins shooed them away, so they could clear up before midnight.

No one was up early the next morning, and it was not with any enthusiasm that they dragged themselves through a lunch of leftovers in order to make the planned rendezvous at two-thirty.

"Let's do this!" June encouraged Cathy as she picked cotton from her jacket. "We don't want to be late. Libby and the twins are going to give us twenty minutes before they arrive, so that we can work out whether or not we should get everyone together."

"Good idea. If it's a disaster, we should know by then," Cathy reasoned.

The sisters sat in the reception area, waiting for the minute hand on the grandfather clock to move round to the appointed time. The main door opened, the bell to alert the reception desk muted by the thickness of the carpet and curtains.

A smart man in his sixties, wearing a full-length trench coat over blazer and neatly pressed trousers, walked towards the hotel desk. They watched him as he spoke to the girl behind the reception desk, Cathy reigning in her impulse to tap him on the shoulder and ask who he thought he was. When he smiled it was as if a hand had clutched Cathy's stomach; in that instant she knew the truth. The smile was just like her mother's grin, his teeth slightly uneven in just the same way hers were. As he lifted his hand to explain something, she saw an indescribable familiarity in the movement, the same tilt of the head her mother would have given.

Neither she nor June said anything, almost holding their breath for fear of giving away who they were. For this instant, they had the upper hand, and she was loath to let it go.

The man who must be their brother moved away, down the corridor towards the bar. The sisters looked at each other, turned and followed him, and Cathy clutched June's arm as they approached. This was it. They had to face the truth about the area of their mother's life of which they had been no part. They had to face this man who could share their inheritance. The meeting with the solicitor had not been reassuring. He showed them a copy of a birth certificate dated sixty-five years ago, when their mother had been just nineteen. There, in black and white, were the facts: Mother Maggie Harrison, father unknown. A boy called Richard George Harrison. There could be no doubt. That was their mother's name, and the baby had their grandfather's middle name as his middle name. And there, at the end of the bar, was that baby — greying hair above eyes as blue as the twins'. His immaculate blazer, shirt and tie, and gleaming shoes complemented his confident step and aura of authority as he genially ordered his drink and made his way to the table by the window.

As June and Cathy approached, he looked up, all confidence draining from his face as a tentative smile acknowledged them. He stood up, and with an unmistakably middle-class accent, enquired, "The daughters of Mrs Mitchell, née Harrison?"

"Yes," they chorused.

"Bob." He stretched out his hand to shake each of theirs. "May I call you June and Cathy?"

They nodded.

"Please sit down — let me get you a drink."

Cathy wanted desperately to dislike him, to find something not right about him, or a way to disbelieve what she'd been told. But every move he made only added to his credibility. She watched as he handed the money over the bar with that smile again. She turned to June, whose eyes had followed hers, and they looked at each other, saying nothing but knowing everything. As she glanced back, she realised that he, too, had been watching. She felt his eyes bore through her. She saw the uncertainty in them, sharply contrasted against his air of self-possession.

Bob came back with their drinks on a tray, and as he carefully placed each on a coaster, his hands shook slightly. As he sat down at the table, Cathy tried to read his body language to find something arrogant in his chin, or his back, or his face. Nothing.

Bob looked into his drink. "I gather you knew nothing about my existence," he said, breaking the silence that was becoming exceedingly awkward.

"No," the two women chorused.

Silence again. What could they say? What Cathy wanted to do was to tell him to go away, forget who he was born to, leave their world the right way up.

"It was a shock to me, as well. I had no idea I had two half-sisters. I didn't even know the circumstances of my adoption, and then there was no information about who my mother was. I was told she died giving birth to me. It seems that was wrong, and I'm so sorry you've only recently lost her. I lost my adoptive mother last year, and I know how painful it must be. It feels strange to have lost two mothers in a year, one I never had the chance to know. I realise you probably wish you still didn't know I exist. I'm trying to make my brain accept that we are what we are. It is a lot to take in, but I find I do want to know. What was she like, my birth mother?"

Cathy turned pleading eyes to June. She knew she couldn't hide the feeling that it was a betrayal to tell this stranger about their own mother. They didn't know what she'd been like at nineteen, had no idea what had happened to her then, or what resemblance that had to the person she had become by the time they could remember her. He was talking about a different person. The one they knew was their father's wife, who would never do anything daring or unconventional. When she married their father, she wore the traditional long white dress, and took on the role of country wife and mother, pillar of village society, member of the WI. What was she like in the days of rock n' roll?

"She was a good mother," volunteered June, "and a good wife. She looked after Dad till the day he died, and she was the sort of person other people went to if they needed to talk about their problems. She could seem a bit old-fashioned at times, and she didn't let us get away with anything, but she was...well, brave, I suppose, when life challenged her."

"How much did you find out about us before the solicitor found you?" broke in Cathy hesitantly, unable to contain her questions any longer.

"I didn't," Bob replied, annoying her with his vagueness. Thankfully, he went on, "It was my grandson wanting to know about names and places that made me start thinking maybe I should try to find out something. I found some papers after my mother died—my adoptive mother. She *was* my mother..." His Adam's apple dipped as he swallowed, but he collected himself quickly. "I found something that told me who my mother was, and there was a letter she wrote when she gave me up for adoption. I'd watched that genealogy documentary programme on the television that traces celebrity family trees, and it got me thinking. I didn't fit on any family tree, other than as an adopted son. I had no roots, no past, no real relatives. I'd never wanted to trace my own mother before that because I loved my adoptive parents, and I didn't want to hurt them. They were wonderful, loving people, who gave me their support all the way through my education and beyond. They WERE my parents, as far as I was concerned. But there it was staring me in the face, that I had someone out there that really was my family by blood, and it got me thinking. It's all there—out there on the internet, you know. You can look up births, deaths, marriages, get copies of certificates, dig into things most people would never have dreamt you could uncover a few years ago. I had my birth certificate, and I just started to find out who was behind the name on the piece of paper. For the first time in my life, I wondered what she looked like, who she really was. There was no way I could find out who my father was, and I began to wonder about that. I thought if I could find her, maybe she would be willing to tell me. I knew she wouldn't have had much choice about giving me up for adoption in the 1940s if she wasn't married, and I suddenly realised what that must have been like for *her*. I'd had a good life, but what had hers been like? Eventually, I found out where she had lived, but I didn't want to confront anyone with who I was. That was last year, and then I was out of action after a car accident, and I put it to the back of my mind. It was only when someone came looking for me that I found out I was too late. She'd died, and a solicitor was trying to trace me because I was mentioned in her will."

After all his words, Bob fell into a wistful silence, looking into his drink again. Cathy saw the sadness in his eyes, and her cold willingness to hate him melted just a little. However, it still didn't excuse him for being able to take away some of what she felt was theirs—at least not in her mind. "So, you saw an opportunity to grab part of what she left, then?" she blurted out.

"Cathy!" exclaimed June, shocked that she should be so blunt, though thinking the same thoughts.

Bob looked up, straight into her eyes, and it was like meeting her mother's stare when she was fifteen—resolute, resigned, probing right into her very thoughts. "No," he said quietly, and with all the control he could muster. He saw her dislike in the tension of her face, knew her mistrust in the tone of her voice, and felt a hostility so strong it was almost tangible. "You don't know me." He looked from one to the other, thinking that the older one seemed more open, more likely to be like the woman who listened to other people's problems.

"No, we don't," Cathy replied, "but we know what you could take away from us."

"I didn't write the will," Bob shrugged, shifting in his seat, as if it were scalding him.

Cathy had no answer.

"Why did you want to meet us?" June asked tentatively.

"I realised I had real relations, half-sisters, people who were also my mother's children. I suppose it was curiosity, as much as anything else. I hoped you would be able to shed some light on what she was like, maybe help me to know her a little, so that I could fill in the blanks I've uncovered. I dared to hope you might even be pleased to see who I was, but that obviously wasn't the case. I understand how you must feel..." Bob trailed off; disappointment audible in his last words.

"You don't need a picture. Look in the mirror," said Cathy abruptly, offering no scrap of comfort in her voice. Looking at him brought all the pain of not being able to look at her mother crashing to the surface. "You have her eyes, her mannerisms."

"Really?" He dared to let the start of a smile creep into the corners of his mouth.

"She's right," added June. "My twins have the same blue eyes."

"You have twins?" he asked, warmed by her offering of this tiny confidence. "So do I!"

"They run in families." *Was it just coincidence?* June tried to remember whether it was passed down through the male or the female line. She tried to grasp the reality of his belonging. So, he had children of his own, a whole family that was related to hers. His children would be cousins of her children—like the one Libby had discovered—and he was their uncle. Her thoughts raced as the image of the man as a thief and outcast was forced to become a vision of the man as family—lost in the circumstances of a by-gone age. It seemed like another age before she heard herself say, "Look, why don't you come to the house, and we can show you some photographs. Maybe it would help." She didn't look in Cathy's direction. She didn't need to. She could feel her tension in the air.

"That's very kind of you," Bob said. "May I call round before I go home tomorrow? Perhaps if we get to know each other a little better, you'll find the situation a little easier."

No chance, thought Cathy, though she said nothing.

Libby, Millie, and Alex tumbled through the front door, each of them feeling uncertain and protective of their mother. Libby took charge, asking at the desk where the bar was and checking that June and Cathy had arrived.

"Now listen, you two. Just keep quiet unless you're asked to speak. OK?"

"We're not babies, Lib," moaned Alex. "I don't know why we have to meet this guy, anyway. Who needs any more relatives? They don't exactly stick around in our family, do they?"

"Alex, for goodness' sake be on your best behaviour! And no swearing!" pleaded Millie. Her brother could be wonderful, but he could be such a pain when things didn't go his way. At this moment in time, she wished he would very quickly grow up as much as she had. Boys were such a liability!

They began walking down the corridor, and Libby suddenly stopped in her tracks. Coming down the stairs was the man she'd met in the flat in London. She couldn't mistake that raven hair—so carefully styled—and the snappy suit for anyone else. How embarrassing! What was he doing here?

"Oh, hello there!" Mike called out as he bounded down the last few stairs, astonished to be confronted by the shock of ginger hair he could not fail to remember. Behind him, she could see a sandy-haired woman walking slowly and deliberately.

"Hello," said Libby, trying to sound cultured. "We met in London, didn't we? I believe you know my friend's father?"

"Yes. Libby, isn't it?"

"Libby?" said a voice behind him. "Did you say Libby?"

Mike turned round as Vicky spoke, and Libby, flanked by the twins, looked at the woman in the floral trousers who'd stopped on the stairs.

"Yes. My name is Libby. Sorry. Should I know you?"

"It may be coincidence, but my name is Vicky. Vicky Thompson."

Alex was pulling "What's going on?" faces at Millie, who was trying to ignore him. She yanked his arm to pull him back across the corridor.

"Oh my God! You're Vicky Thompson? The Vicky I've been in touch with?"

"Well, if you're the Libby I've been in touch with."

"I am. What are you doing here?"

"Long story, but our father is in the bar. We're staying here for the weekend. What are you doing here?"

"We live in the area. Our mother and our aunt are in the bar, too."

"Well, I could do with a drink!" Mike said. "I'll go and find Dad while you two have a chat." With that, he marched down the corridor, not wanting to be embroiled in female small talk.

Libby became aware of the twins behind her. "Oh, Vicky, these are my brother and sister. This is Millie and this is Alex."

"Hello, you two. Are you twins, like my brother Mike and me?"

"Yes," they chorused.

"Look, shall we go through to the bar? We can find our parents, then have a proper chat," suggested Vicky.

What they saw as they entered the bar was not quite what they expected. Vicky walked towards her father, Libby headed for her mother, and they found themselves aiming for the same table under the bay window. Several pairs of eyes darted from one person to another, trying to make sense of the tableau before them. Nobody spoke, then everyone seemed to speak at once.

"So, who is your father?"

"Are you going to introduce us, Dad?"

"Mum, is this your brother?"

"Who's that with you, Libby?"

Mike, who had already been introduced to Cathy and June, stepped in between the newcomers and the table. "Right. Let's sort this out, shall we? I'll start. I'm Mike Thompson. This is my sister, Vicky, and this is our dad, Bob Thompson."

Libby took her cue from Mike. "Well, I'm Libby Braithwaite. This is my brother, Alex, and my sister, Millie, and this is my mum, June. This is my mum's sister, Cathy Mitchell."

A chorus of "hello" followed, then another awkward silence.

"So," began Vicky. "Dad, are these your sisters? Are we all cousins?"

"Yes, it would seem so," said Bob.

Vicky stepped forward, determined to make this meeting work, for Bob's sake. She held out her hand, thinking that maybe kissing on both cheeks would be a bit premature. "I'm so pleased to meet you," she said with a genuine smile that made the two women warm to her, instinctively.

"Hello, Vicky," June said. "Your dad has just been telling us about you. I gather that, like me, you're a teacher."

"Oh, you teach as well! What a coincidence, or maybe not such a coincidence!" Vicky beamed at June, noticing out of the corner of her eye that Cathy did not seem nearly so willing to reach out. "Of course, my brother doesn't teach. He's a big shot in finance in London. He's much more interested in the cut and thrust of the business world than I am." She could sense Mike wanting to kick her in the ankle, but she persevered. "So, what do you do, Cathy? Are you a teacher, too?"

"No. Never. I have my own property business over in Perth." It dawned on Mike and Vicky that the accent meant Perth, Australia, not Scotland.

Vicky laughed. "So, you two are the same as we are—one teaching and one in business. Fascinating, isn't it, when you start to see the genes at work?" She immediately regretted the comment, thinking that drawing the comparison may have been a step too far. Did she see Cathy flinch?

"Well Libby has broken the mould," chipped in Millie. "She's going to be a wonderful doctor. Alex wants to be a vet, like his great grandfather, and I have no idea what I'm going to do."

They were all aware that they were desperately avoiding the one subject they all wanted to talk about. It was June who decided to make a stand. "Come and sit down, all of you," she invited. "Grab a couple of those stools over there, Alex. Now, the fact is that—strange and new as it seems to all of us—we are related. There is an uncanny likeness between you, Bob, and our mother, and between you, Mike, and the photograph we found of your biological grandfather. Neither our mother nor our father was dark-haired, but the pilot was. Was your mother dark-haired, too? Did you get your colouring from her?"

"No. She was kind of mousy, actually," answered Mike. "She used to joke that I must be a throwback, and she and Dad never hid the fact that they were both adopted, so we thought nothing of it. It feels weird, suddenly putting a name and a face to where it came from, though."

"You're lucky it's dark and not ginger," Libby commented, with feeling.

"What's it like living in Australia?" asked Vicky.

"Warm," said Cathy, as it was the first word that came into her head, having felt cold ever since she arrived in the country. "You can plan to do something and know you'll be able to do it because we don't get much rain unless it's winter. We have beautiful beaches, lots of them, and wineries, and fantastic places to eat, and life's good, actually." As she spoke, she realised she felt defensive of her lifestyle, and she did enjoy it. She felt a pang of what seemed to be homesickness. "I'm going back soon. That's one reason for the party, though the other was June's impending fiftieth birthday."

"You're leaving? We won't have the chance to get to know each other very well, then, will we? That's a shame," Vicky said, shaking her head sadly. "Perhaps you'll come back for another visit, and we can meet up again."

"I dare say I'll be back at some stage, though I'm hoping I can tempt my sister into coming out to visit me instead, next time." Cathy gave June a friendly nudge.

"You've heard the will, then?" June brought the conversation back to the point.

Bob spoke up, "Yes, I have. Look, I didn't seek this. I don't need it. I want you to know that I have no intention of turning you out of your home or taking away from you what our mother should have left to you two. I just wanted to see it for myself. I had a mother and father. I have a family. I was born into yours, but we parted almost a lifetime ago, and

I have nothing to regret, other than wishing I could have told her she gave me the chance of a wonderful upbringing in a loving home, and I wanted for nothing. I would have liked to have rid her of any feelings of guilt and sadness, though I know I couldn't have wiped out all those years of missing me she must have held on to." He coughed into his hand, fighting for control as his throat tightened round the words he'd planned to calmly say. "I would have liked to thank her. She must have carried her past with her, and that's what I think is the worst thing about all of this. When I've thought about it, I've realised I had the chance to be happy, and hopefully so did she, but behind her happiness was the loss of a man she loved and a child she carried. For that, my heart goes out to her." He looked down into his drink, not wanting to say so much that his emotion came to the surface.

"It was hard, finding all of those things in the loft," said June. "We found letters she wrote to her parents while she was in Wales. It seems they didn't even go to see her while she was there. They must have been determined to carry on as normal, to wipe out the shame of her pregnancy. But she was happy with our dad, you know. She met him some time later because he worked here, at the Hall, as Estate Manager. Did you know that?"

Bob looked around him with wonder. "No. I'm glad she found someone else and had a family she could keep. You must have been all the more precious to her."

"We know she loved us." Cathy was slowly thawing towards this stranger who seemed to be able to empathise in a way she had not expected him to. She had to admit that he didn't seem to be the villain she'd painted in her mind. She might even have to accept that he seemed a decent man. Calling him her brother was going to be pushing his luck, though.

"There is one person you haven't met today," Vicky ventured. "I have a son, George. We call him Georgie. I'm not married, and Mum and Dad have certainly not sent me away. I feel very lucky, hearing your mother's story—my grandmother's story, I suppose. I didn't have a relationship with Georgie's father, and falling pregnant, becoming a single parent, was not something I planned, but there was no question of me giving away my son. I have a job I love, I have my son, and I have my precious dad. He's a good man, my dad." She turned on her heel and headed out of the room.

"Excuse me," said Mike as he followed her, knowing she would need a brotherly hug. She was right. Their father was a good man. These two women were lucky that he was their brother. He hoped one day they would realise that.

Alex and Millie quietly withdrew to the reception area, feeling that now was not the time to voice an opinion on anything, and they were best out of the way if emotions were going to start flying.

Libby reached over the back of the chair to give her mum an encouraging pat on the shoulders. "I'm going to leave you three to talk," she said. "Mum, I'll be in reception when you're ready to leave. I'll drive. I like Vicky," she said to Bob. "I'd like to keep in touch if that's OK."

"Of course, it is." Bob smiled at her, and she saw the same crinkle at the corner of his eyes as her gran had. It was uncanny, unnerving, and wonderful, all at the same time.

Libby left them to it, hoping they would find in each other something approaching at least a friendship as they got to know each other. By the time she got to reception, Vicky had been up to her room and come back down again, and the cousins were sitting on the blue leather sofas, discussing their parents.

Vicky waved her over to sit next to her. "I'm glad you've joined us, Libby. Look, I know you were delving into the family history, just as I was. I have to ask you something. Your mum's maiden name was Mitchell, wasn't it?"

"Yes."

"So, her dad's surname was Mitchell."

"Yes. Why? What's that got to do with anything?"

"I'm not sure, but I think I might have uncovered an incredible coincidence. You see, my dad wasn't the only one who was adopted. One thing he and Mum had in common was that they were both adopted, but I've recently been reminded that Mum was adopted by her grandparents, her mother's parents, because her parents both died."

"Whew! How unlucky can you get?" chimed in Millie, while Alex had, by now, plugged in his earphones and was listening to music his mother would hate, drumming his fingers on the arm of the sofa.

"What I have only found out since I started digging is that her real father was a man called Phillip Mitchell. Does that ring a bell with you? Could it be the same family?"

"Oh, that just seems too much of a coincidence, doesn't it? Surely it can't be the same one, but my granddad did have a brother called Phillip, who was killed in an accident, we were told. Granddad said he was a lovely brother, and he really missed him because there had only been the two of them, after a third one was killed during the war. Colin, I think he was. Gran knew the stories, but to be honest, we didn't take much notice of them when we were younger."

"My mum was an orphan, because her mum died in childbirth, and her dad was killed in an accident. Her mum's parents adopted her and took her to Cornwall, where they lived. I think there's a possibility that her dad was your grandfather's brother, so we are related on both sides of the family. I can't work out what that's called off the top of my head!" Vicky took a deep breath. "Whew! Dad had no idea what his parents' names were, and even if he'd known, he wouldn't have known who his mother went on to marry. The trouble with doing this family history stuff is that you start to unravel the complicated stories that weave people's lives together, and sometimes it might be better to leave well alone!" Vicky and Libby shared a knowing smile.

"Just think. If the pilot had come back and married Gran, we wouldn't be here!" Millie's brain had obviously been working it all out.

"Hmmm. So, are you going to tell them all this, Vicky, or do we each tell our own parent?" asked Libby.

"I don't think they can handle any more right now, do you? Best to leave it to another day. It might come out when they look at the photos tomorrow, but if not, we could tell them later," Vicky said. "Dad has had a tough year, one way or another, and if your mum and your aunt give him a chance, they'll probably find they're alike in some ways, and maybe they'll get to like each other. At least now everyone knows the truth."

"So do we," said Libby, "and I'm glad. Gran's past doesn't have to be a secret anymore, and your dad knows who his parents were."

"And Mike knows why he has dark hair, when both of his parents were fair! It wasn't the milkman, after all!" joked Vicky, not that they had ever suspected their mother of being unfaithful to their father.

Back in the bar, the conversation had run its course for the first meeting. Bob had seen similarities between Cathy and Mike in their itchiness to move about, their tendency to sound brisk and something across the eyebrows that seemed familiar. In June, he saw an older version of Vicky, though different to look at, as Vicky was like her mum. Thoughtful, open to new ideas, a natural warmth and a feeling that they were both the kind of people you wanted around in a crisis. Bob thought they would get on if they had the chance.

They agreed that Bob and Vicky would come to June's house for coffee in the morning before setting off home. It was clear that Mike would not join them; he had to be back in London.

They parted stiffly, Cathy barely able to shake Bob's hand, so eerily like her mother's, while June held it in both of hers, feeling his trembling. Cathy couldn't let down her guard because to do so was to let in too much sadness, too much loss, and she didn't want to feel it. Right now, Bob Thompson was not going to worm his way into her heart, however hard he tried. As far as she was concerned, he was an intruder into their world, a manifestation of the past existing in the present, and potentially determining part of the future. She certainly wouldn't acknowledge what others would observe, had she and Mike stood side by side—they were so obviously related. In their mannerisms and their attitudes, they were so alike they would probably clash, had they ever spent time together.

Chapter Thirty-Five

With Mike having roared his way out of the car park, Vicky and Bob went up to pack their cases and make their way to the smallholding, which Bob had shown Vicky and Mike from the road. As they reached the five-bar gate, they heard the dogs begin to bark and hoped they were not on the loose. They walked through the smaller gate, to the right, and faced a decision. Front door, round to the left, behind the wall, or straight on, where the back door opened onto the yard. As it was their first visit, they felt they should head for the front door, but just as they turned, a voice called out from the distance.

"Hello there! Come on down to the back door. No one uses the front door unless they're delivering the milk, or they don't know us." Alex appeared with the dogs on leads. "Don't worry about the dogs. They're perfectly harmless." He guessed these two were not used to dogs, judging by the body language, so he took them in ahead of the visitors and shut them in the utility room until they'd gone through the kitchen and on to the lounge, where June came to meet them.

"Bob, Vicky, come on in," June welcomed. "Sit yourselves down near the fire. Can I offer you a cup of tea or coffee?"

"Thank you. Black coffee would be good," answered Bob.

"Could I just have a glass of water, please? I try to avoid caffeine," said Vicky.

"Fine. Let me take your coats."

"I'll do the drinks, shall I?" offered Cathy. "You can get the photos out, if you like."

"Right," June agreed. "I'll just put these coats in the hall."

The formalities over, June brought the old albums with photos of their mother as a young woman, and photos of their grandparents for

Bob to see. He tried to fix the memory of them in his brain, but he knew that, try as he might, he wouldn't keep it all there.

"I know it's an imposition, and say if it would be too much trouble, but is there any chance I could have a copy of some of these for my grandson, George? I'd like to be able to pass something on to show him who his ancestors were. I don't mind if it's just a photocopy if he can see the faces. It's just somehow important to see where your nose came from, whose eyes you have, who has the same build, the same way of standing or sitting. You see, I've never had that. I'd like Vicky and George to have that. It joins you to the generations that came before you, doesn't it, and to the ones that come after you?"

"I'd never thought of that," Cathy commented. "I suppose we just took it for granted. It must be strange not knowing, though I suppose if you go back far enough, they didn't even have photos to record what their parents looked like. It's just that now we have so many that it's hard to imagine a time without them."

"I'll get some copies made for you," offered June. "Libby's going back to Newcastle, but I'll see if she'd like some, too, since she seems to have been into this family tree business. Look, this is Mum and Dad before we arrived. I think that man in the background is Dad's brother."

"Was he called Phillip, by any chance?" Vicky asked.

"Well yes, he was," June answered, eyebrows raised "How did you know that?"

When Vicky told them what she had already shared with Libby, they were all amazed. How could life be full of so many coincidences? It was almost as if there was some invisible web holding them all together.

Cathy thought, *If we were religious, we'd start saying 'God works in mysterious ways' or 'He has a plan.'* She didn't know what she believed, but she left going to church to June.

By the time they'd pored over more photos of relatives and Cathy and June as children, it was almost lunch time, and Bob and Vicky had to be on their way. As they rose to go, Bob shook the sisters' hands and thanked them profusely for letting him see the photographs, his genuine gratitude evident in his tone and the sparkle in his eyes.

As Vicky shook hands, she decided that she would have to take a leap of faith. "Look, you haven't had much time this weekend, so how about if I keep in touch, and we try to get you together again later in the year, maybe in the summer holiday?"

"Oh, that's a great idea, Vicky," began June, a need to know this newly discovered brother stirring inside her and welcoming the offer. "Cathy will be going back to Perth, of course, so she won't be able to contact you as easily as I can, but maybe Bob and I could talk to each other on the phone in a couple of weeks?"

"I'd like that," said Bob. "I'd like to get to know you if you would be prepared to give it a try. I know it's a shock for you, that we share a mother, and to be honest, I'm still not sure I've really got my head round having a whole other family. It's going to take us all time to adjust to what we know now, but maybe we could start to fill in some of the gaps, and maybe at least our children could get to know their cousins."

"I could keep in touch with Libby through Facebook," Vicky offered, "or email. I'd like Georgie to meet you all so that he has a chance to be part of a wider family. I haven't had cousins before, so I'm beginning to like the idea that I've got some." She grinned at Libby and the twins, who met her enthusiasm with friendly choruses of "Yes." She didn't think Mike would want to be bothered, but she didn't say so. He had a very full life as it was, and Vicky was very aware that she made him keep in contact with her, whether he could be bothered or not! He did that man-thing of not keeping a record of when birthdays were, and she had to remind him. He had a secretary to organise his work appointments for him, and friends who messaged him or phoned him, so that he kept up with the social life. He'd been bemoaning, lately, that some of them were now married and starting to have children, which ruined their ability to join him on a weekend spree. He had no intention of tying himself down yet.

Bob knew he would probably never see this house again, whatever the will said, but he hoped Vicky and Georgie would get to know their new family and future generations would be able to acknowledge all the people that had been parents to him. He had a feeling that Cathy would never be close, but maybe she would be prepared to meet his family again when she came over. June seemed to be a more kindred spirit; he'd felt a genuine warmth and compassion in her, and he hoped she would eventually feel that they could be in touch without Vicky's contribution. He thought he really might phone her now and then and see how it went.

Chapter Thirty-Six

June put the finishing touches to an interactive presentation for her literature class. She sat back, satisfied that it would spark a lively discussion of women's rights. It had been a topic of heated debate at home since the family had met Bob. Libby had challenged Cathy about injustice on both sides of the world, with Aboriginal children taken from their mothers in Australia for all the wrong reasons.

"You're right, Libby. The world hasn't been a fair place, but your generation can keep making it better. Don't ever let yourself be treated badly, just because you're a woman." Cathy's heartfelt response cemented the growing bond between aunt and niece.

As June packed away her laptop, she just had time to make a phone call before she had to collect Millie from her friend's.

Vicky was marking a pile of essays when her mobile rang. Irritated, she picked it up impatiently, ready to curse anyone trying to sell her something. She was glad she said no more than "Hello," when June's now-familiar voice spoke.

"Hi, Vicky! I just thought I'd give you a ring, to see how everyone is."

"We're not too bad, thanks, June. I don't know about you, but I'll be glad when the end of term comes!"

"Absolutely, Vicky. Look, I was wondering if you'd like to bring Georgie up for a visit the week after next while he's on his school holiday? We're going to spend a few days at the coast, and I've rented a cottage big enough for all of us, but Libby has other plans. There's a spare room if you'd like to join us. You could do with a break!"

"Oh, that would be wonderful, June! He's desperate to meet his other family! Dad has been quizzed non-stop about who you are, what you look like, what you do." Vicky laughed. "Dad says Georgie started this with his family tree curiosity, so he's to blame! The whole truth would be a bit much for him at his age, but he's been boasting about you at school."

"I'd like to meet him, too, Vicky. So would the twins. They're quite taken with the idea of a young cousin."

"It's a shame Dad wouldn't be able to come, too."

"A bit too much for him, I would think. He sounded quite frail when I phoned last week."

"Yes, I'm afraid so. I don't think he'd be up to the journey now. I'd only be able to stay for a night or two, though he's well cared for. I just feel I need to be nearby now."

"It must have been such a shock," June said, "getting the diagnosis when you got back from here."

"Yes. I think he knew there was something wrong. That's why it was so urgent to meet you. He'll fight—I know he will—but I think he's weaker than he was. Knowing he only has a few months to a year has sapped his strength."

"I'm glad we made it down to London last month. I feel as if we've really got to know each other now." June paused. She had found her brother, only to face losing him so soon. Time was so precious. "He's a decent man, your father, isn't he?"

"One of the best, June. I've been very lucky." Quickly changing the subject, Vicky added, "I'm looking forward to meeting up with Libby again soon. She's going to bring her version of the family tree down to me, and we're going to compare. It's turned into a mammoth beast!"

"I'm so glad you two have hit it off! Good luck with that tree! Your generation will certainly have a truer picture than we ever did. The more we find out, the more complicated it is! Well, I must go now, but I'll send you details, and tell Bob I'll phone again at the end of the week. Take care."

"Thanks, June. See you soon, with a bit of luck! Bye!"

Epilogue

"Healing is a matter of time, but it is sometimes also a matter of opportunity." - Hippocrates

The christening of Jim's daughter, Kate, took place on a beautiful Sunday. As her proud Godmother, Cathy was delighted to hold her, but relieved to hand her back before friends and family gathered for lunch in one of Perth's prestigious restaurants.

Cathy had returned in time for the birth, relieved that her business had survived in Jim's capable hands. She made sure she visited him and his wife in the days after the baby was born, laden with flowers and gifts. She found she liked their company and surprised them by making time to have them round to dinner.

Gratefully, Cathy declared, "Jim, I can't thank you enough. I know what I owe you. Look, how would you feel about permanent promotion? What about appointing a deputy to help you? I need to step back a bit, give you the freedom to use your experience."

"I'd be delighted," replied Jim. "I've enjoyed being in charge!" His eyes twinkled with a mischievous smile, though beneath the humour was a truth he would not deny.

She made time for her female friends, too, and they began to find a softer Cathy, less in a hurry than the one they had known before. As she sat among them at the christening lunch, the conversation inevitably turned to Robin's impending marriage.

"Have you been invited to the wedding?" ventured Karen.

"Yes, but I won't turn up at the ceremony. I hope they'll be very happy. I'm not the same person I was when I left here in December. I hardly recognise myself, so I don't see any point in dragging myself through painful memories."

"What do you mean, not the same person? You look pretty much the same to me!" laughed Karen, her smile fading, as she read Cathy's serious face. "What's changed, Cathy?"

"I know how driven I've been over the past few years. Somehow, I lost the person I was when I was younger and going back to England gave me the chance to find that bit of myself again. I've missed slumming around in my jeans, running free across the fields. I've been so busy being in control, to feel safe, that I've never let myself relax and just be. It's time I did that here." Cathy pulled on her jacket. "I'll explain when we meet for coffee next week."

Cathy knew it was time to shift her focus. She'd begun to heal by going back, but there was a way to go, and the rest of it had to be done here, in her real world, where she belonged. She needed to talk about how she had felt all those years ago, when she ran away across the world, but not here, not now. When they were on their own, she would share her truth with her friend.

She didn't mind June being in touch with Bob, but she had no wish to become enmeshed in his life. He couldn't be part of her future, any more than he was part of her past. It was too late for that. Too much time and too many miles apart, but at least now the past had been articulated, not denied. That denial had corrupted the past, but now they'd brought it out of the shadows, into the light, perhaps it could become a memory for future generations, just as it had been for her mother. Perhaps there could be a new continuum of past, present, and future.

Walking along the Swan River towards Point Walter, Cathy contemplated how many people had moved along these shores, part of the waves of newcomers who'd shaped the place she now called home. As she reached the seat dedicated to the "stolen generation," she thought about what it must have been like for all the mothers whose children had been taken from them, and all the children who'd never known their real families. She remembered Libby's passionate outburst. She read the words on the plaque:

"The practice of taking children left a legacy of trauma and loss..."

For the first time since she'd become an Australian citizen, she found an unfamiliar empathy stirring inside her. She'd gone back to the land of her own ancestors, only to find that the land no longer bound her to it. As she looked out across the water at the familiar silhouette of the city, she realised that what mattered was the past she carried within her, a past that time could not change. Her mother had kept her sadness and her loss to herself, but, like so many of her generation, she'd gone to her grave with that trauma unresolved and the sorrow never wiped away.

That evening, on her laptop, Cathy listened to the testimonies of the children who were part of the "stolen generation." There was a lot wrong with the world but thank goodness it had changed. Their experiences seared her heart. "Half-caste" children had been forcibly removed in an attempt to dilute their brown skin in the future. How could that have been seen as right? How could it have been right to take away a baby born of love to a woman who had already lost the man who fathered it? She felt the weight of being a woman in a world where women had, for so long, been victims of hypocrisy and twisted morality. Somewhere in her head, those Aboriginal women and her own mother blended into one huge, tangled barb of loss. She would understand, next May, her country's "Sorry Day." She only wished there could be another, across the world, for all those women who wept for the children taken from them.

She thought about the fact that none of the hundreds of Aboriginal languages contains a word for time, and what has been translated as "The Dreaming" is seen as going from the past to the present to the future, all at once. She felt as if she'd done just that. It was as if she'd been in a sea, waves of past and present crashing over each other, reality finally washing away the illusion of truth she thought she had. She would finally shrug off the shadow of her own past and slow the tide of the future flowing towards her. It was just a matter of time.

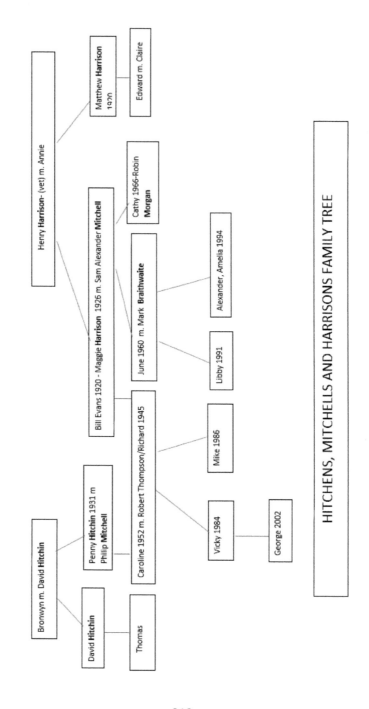

Henry **Harrison**- (vet) m. Annie

Matthew **Harrison**
1920

Edward m. Claire

Bill Evans 1920 - Maggie **Harrison** 1926 m. Sam Alexander **Mitchell**

Cathy 1966-Robin **Morgan**

June 1960 m. Mark **Braithwaite**

Alexander, Amelia 1994

Libby 1991

Caroline 1952 m. Robert Thompson/Richard 1945

Mike 1986

Vicky 1984

George 2002

Bronwyn m. David **Hitchin**

Penny **Hitchin** 1931 m Philip **Mitchell**

David **Hitchin**

Thomas

HITCHENS, MITCHELLS AND HARRISONS FAMILY TREE

Jackie Hales is a member of the Society of Authors, whose debut novel *Shadows of Time* was the fulfilment of an ambition nurtured during her working life as a teacher, inspired by her research into her own and others' family histories. She has been writing as a hobby since childhood, beginning to contribute to poetry anthologies in her undergraduate days and being a Poetry Guild national semi-finalist in the 1990s. She has also written short stories for friends, family, and students. Since retiring, she has contributed to "Poetry Archive Now" (2020), with *20-20 Vision*, uploaded to YouTube, and has had poetry and flash fiction published online by Flash Fiction North. One of her flash fictions is to appear in an anthology, having been selected from entries during the Morecambe Festival. She had a creative memoir, *Shelf Life*, published by Dear Damsels in 2019, a precursor to collaborating with her sister on a creative non-fiction memoir *Remnants of War*, published in 2021. She writes a blog about her walks and thoughts in the Yorkshire and Somerset countryside.

Twitter account: Jackie Meekums Hales, writer (@jackieihales) / Twitter

Blog: Jotting Jax

Facebook author page: Jackie Meekums Hales

20-20 Vision by Jackie Hales – YouTube